Contents

Nonfiction Reading Practice Is Important

Research indicates that more than 80 percent of what people read and write is nonfiction text. Newspapers, magazines, directions on new products, application forms, and how-to manuals are just some of the types of nonfiction reading material we encounter on a daily basis. As students move through the grades, an increasing amount of time is spent reading expository text for subjects such as science and social studies. Most reading comprehension sections on state and national tests are nonfiction.

Each Unit Has...

A Teacher Resource Page

Vocabulary words for all three levels are given. The vocabulary lists include proper nouns and content-specific words, as well as other challenging words.

A Visual Aid

The visual aid represents the topic for the unit. It is intended to build interest in the topic. Reproduce the visual on an overhead transparency or photocopy it for each student.

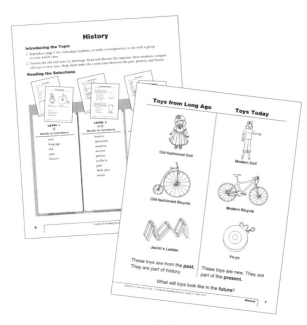

Articles at Three Reading Levels

Each unit presents three articles on the same topic. The articles progress in difficulty from easiest (Level 1) to hardest (Level 3). An icon indicates the level of the article—Level 1 (■), Level 2 (■ ■), Level 3 (■ ■ ■). Each article contains new vocabulary and ideas to incorporate into classroom discussion. The Level 1 article gives readers a core vocabulary and a basic understanding of the topic. More challenging vocabulary words are used as the level of the article increases. Interesting details also change or increase in the Levels 2 and 3 articles.

Level 1

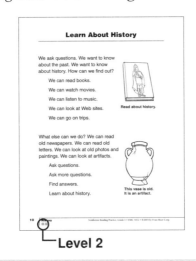

Level 2

Level 3

Readability

All of the articles in this series have been edited for readability. Readability formulas, which are mathematical calculations, are considered to be one way of predicting reading ease. The Flesch-Kincaid and Fry Graph formulas were used to check for readability. These formulas count and factor in three variables: the number of words, syllables, and sentences in a passage to determine the reading level. When appropriate, proper nouns and content-specific terms were discounted in determining readability levels for the articles in this book.

Nonfiction Reading Practice, Grade 1 • EMC 3312 • ©2003 by Evan-Moor Corp.

Student Comprehension Pages

A vocabulary/comprehension page follows each article. There are three multiple-choice questions that provide practice with the types of questions that are generally used on standardized reading tests. The bonus question is intended to elicit higher-level thinking skills.

Level 1

Level 2

Level 3

Additional Resources

Six graphic organizers to extend comprehension are also included in the book. (See page 4 for suggestions for use.

Famous Person

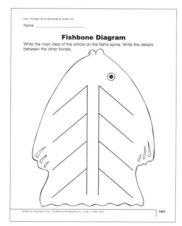

Fishbone Diagram

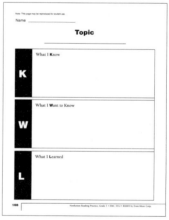

KWL Chart

Sequence Chart

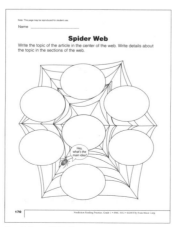

Spider Web

Word Quilt

How to Use *Nonfiction Reading Practice*

Planning Instruction

The units in this book do not need to be taught in sequential order. Choose the units that align with your curriculum or with student interests.

- For whole-group instruction, introduce the unit to the total class. Provide each student with an article at the appropriate reading level. Guide students as they read the articles. You may want to have students read with partners. Then conduct a class discussion to share the different information learned.

- For small-group instruction, choose an article at the appropriate reading level for each group. The group reads the article with teacher guidance and discusses the information presented.

- The articles may also be used to assist readers in moving from less difficult to more challenging reading material. After building vocabulary and familiarity with the topic at the appropriate level, students may be able to successfully read the article at the next level of difficulty.

Presenting a Unit

1. Before reading the articles, make an overhead transparency of the visual aid or reproduce it for individual student use. Use the visual to engage student interest in the topic, present vocabulary, and build background that will aid in comprehension. This step is especially important for visual learners.

2. Present vocabulary that may be difficult to decode or understand. A list of suggested vocabulary words for each article is given on the teacher resource page. Where possible, connect these words to the visual aid.

3. Present and model several appropriate reading strategies that aid in comprehension of the expository text. You may wish to make an overhead transparency of the reading strategies checklist on page 5 or reproduce it for students to refer to as they read.

4. You may want to use one of the graphic organizers provided on pages 166–171. Make an overhead transparency, copy the organizer onto the board or chart paper, or reproduce it for students. Record information learned to help students process and organize the information.

5. Depending on the ability levels of the students, the comprehension/vocabulary pages may be completed as a group or as independent practice. It is always advantageous to share and discuss answers as a group so that students correct misconceptions. An answer key is provided at the back of this book.

Name _____

Reading Checklist

Directions: Check off the reading hints that you use to understand the story.

Before I Read

_____ I think about what I already know.

_____ I think about what I want to learn.

_____ I predict what is going to happen.

_____ I read the title for clues.

_____ I look at the pictures for clues.

While I Read

_____ I stop and retell to check what I remember.

_____ I reread parts that are confusing.

_____ I read the captions under the pictures.

_____ I make pictures of the story in my mind.

_____ I figure out ways to understand hard words.

After I Read

_____ I think about what I have just read.

_____ I speak, draw, and write about what I read.

_____ I reread favorite parts.

_____ I reread to find details.

_____ I look back at the story to find answers to questions.

History

Introducing the Topic

1. Reproduce page 7 for individual students, or make a transparency to use with a group or your whole class.

2. Present the old and new toy drawings. Read and discuss the captions. Have students compare old toys to new toys. Help them make the connection between the past, present, and future.

Reading the Selections

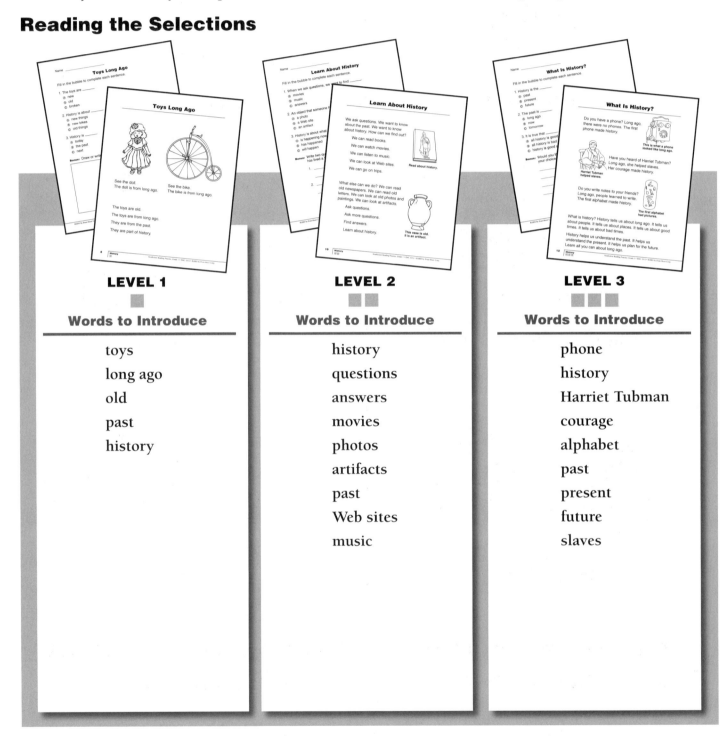

LEVEL 1	LEVEL 2	LEVEL 3
Words to Introduce	**Words to Introduce**	**Words to Introduce**
toys	history	phone
long ago	questions	history
old	answers	Harriet Tubman
past	movies	courage
history	photos	alphabet
	artifacts	past
	past	present
	Web sites	future
	music	slaves

Toys from Long Ago	**Toys Today**

Old-fashioned Doll	**Modern Doll**

Old-fashioned Bicycle	**Modern Bicycle**

Jacob's Ladder	**Yo-yo**
These toys are from the **past**. They are part of history.	These toys are new. They are part of the **present**.

What will toys look like in the **future**?

Toys Long Ago

See the doll.
The doll is from long ago.

See the bike.
The bike is from long ago.

The toys are old.

The toys are from long ago.

They are from the past.

They are part of history.

Nonfiction Reading Practice, Grade 1 • EMC 3312 • ©2003 by Evan-Moor Corp.

Name _____

Toys Long Ago

Fill in the bubble to complete each sentence.

1. The toys are _____.

    Ⓐ new

    Ⓑ old

    Ⓒ broken

2. History is about _____.

    Ⓐ new things

    Ⓑ new bikes

    Ⓒ old things

3. **History** is _____.

    Ⓐ today

    Ⓑ the past

    Ⓒ next

Bonus: Draw or write about a toy you play with today.

Learn About History

We ask questions. We want to know about the past. We want to know about history. How can we find out?

Read about history.

We can read books.

We can watch movies.

We can listen to music.

We can look at Web sites.

We can go on trips.

What else can we do? We can read old newspapers. We can read old letters. We can look at old photos and paintings. We can look at artifacts.

Ask questions.

Ask more questions.

Find answers.

Learn about history.

**This vase is old.
It is an artifact.**

Nonfiction Reading Practice, Grade 1 • EMC 3312 • ©2003 by Evan-Moor Corp.

Name _____

Learn About History

Fill in the bubble to complete each sentence.

1. When we ask questions, we want to find _____.
   - Ⓐ movies
   - Ⓑ music
   - Ⓒ answers

2. An object that someone has made or used is _____.
   - Ⓐ a photo
   - Ⓑ a Web site
   - Ⓒ an artifact

3. History is about what _____.
   - Ⓐ is happening now
   - Ⓑ has happened
   - Ⓒ will happen

Bonus: Write two questions you would like to ask someone who has lived a long time.

1. _____

_____

2. _____

_____

What Is History?

Do you have a phone? Long ago, there were no phones. The first phone made history.

This is what a phone looked like long ago.

Harriet Tubman helped slaves.

Have you heard of Harriet Tubman? Long ago, she helped slaves. Her courage made history.

Do you write notes to your friends? Long ago, people learned to write. The first alphabet made history.

The first alphabet had pictures.

What is history? History tells us about long ago. It tells us about people. It tells us about places. It tells us about good times. It tells us about bad times.

History helps us understand the past. It helps us understand the present. It helps us plan for the future. Learn all you can about long ago.

Nonfiction Reading Practice, Grade 1 • EMC 3312 • ©2003 by Evan-Moor Corp.

Name _____

What Is History?

Fill in the bubble to complete each sentence.

1. History is the _____.
   - Ⓐ past
   - Ⓑ present
   - Ⓒ future

2. The **past** is _____.
   - Ⓐ now
   - Ⓑ long ago
   - Ⓒ tomorrow

3. It is true that _____.
   - Ⓐ all history is good
   - Ⓑ all history is bad
   - Ⓒ history is good and bad

Bonus: Would you like to visit the past or the future? Write about your choice.

_____

_____

_____

_____

The Library

Introducing the Topic

1. Reproduce page 15 for individual students, or make a transparency to use with a group or your whole class.

2. Present the picture of the inside of a library. Read and discuss the different areas of a library. Ask students how this library is like and unlike the library in their school.

Reading the Selections

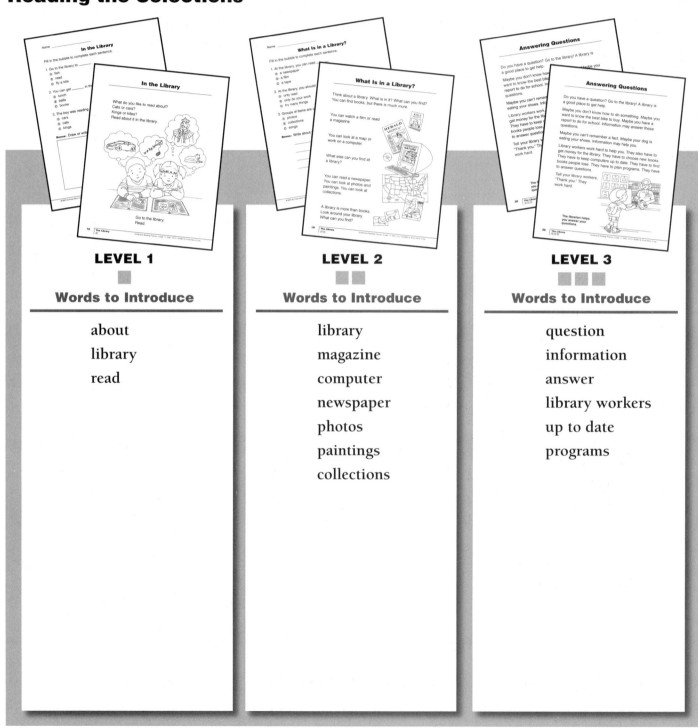

LEVEL 1

Words to Introduce

about

library

read

LEVEL 2

Words to Introduce

library

magazine

computer

newspaper

photos

paintings

collections

LEVEL 3

Words to Introduce

question

information

answer

library workers

up to date

programs

Nonfiction Reading Practice, Grade 1 • EMC 3312 • ©2003 by Evan-Moor Corp.

The Library

computer
station

books

study table

card catalog

check-out
counter

The library is also called the media center. How is this
library like your library? How is it different?

In the Library

What do you like to read about?
Cats or cars?
Kings or kites?
Read about it in the library.

Go to the library.
Read.

Name _____

In the Library

Fill in the bubble to complete each sentence.

1. You go to the library to _____.
   - Ⓐ fish
   - Ⓑ read
   - Ⓒ fly a kite

2. You can find _____ in the library.
   - Ⓐ lunch
   - Ⓑ balls
   - Ⓒ books

3. The boy was reading about _____.
   - Ⓐ cars
   - Ⓑ cats
   - Ⓒ kings

Bonus: Draw or write about the book you like best.

What Is in a Library?

Think about a library. What is in it? What can you find? You can find books, but there is much more.

You can watch a film or read a magazine.

You can look at a map or work on a computer.

What else can you find in a library?

You can read a newspaper. You can look at photos and paintings. You can look at collections.

A library is more than books. Look around your library. What can you find?

Nonfiction Reading Practice, Grade 1 • EMC 3312 • ©2003 by Evan-Moor Corp.

Name _____

What Is in a Library?

Fill in the bubble to complete each sentence.

1. At the library, you can read _____.
   - Ⓐ a newspaper
   - Ⓑ a film
   - Ⓒ a tape

2. At the library, you should _____.
   - Ⓐ only read
   - Ⓑ only do your work
   - Ⓒ try many things

3. Groups of items are called _____.
   - Ⓐ photos
   - Ⓑ collections
   - Ⓒ songs

Bonus: Write about your favorite thing to do at the library.

_____

_____

_____

_____

Answering Questions

Do you have a question? Go to the library! A library is a good place to get help.

Maybe you don't know how to do something. Maybe you want to know the best bike to buy. Maybe you have a report to do for school. Information may answer these questions.

Maybe you can't remember a fact. Maybe your dog is eating your shoes. Information may help you.

Library workers work hard to help you. They also have to get money for the library. They have to choose new books. They have to keep computers up to date. They have to find books people lose. They have to plan programs. They have to answer questions.

Tell your library workers, "Thank you." They work hard.

The librarian helps you answer your questions.

Nonfiction Reading Practice, Grade 1 • EMC 3312 • ©2003 by Evan-Moor Corp.

Name _____

Answering Questions

Fill in the bubble to complete each sentence.

1. Library workers will _____.
   - Ⓐ do your reports for school
   - Ⓑ help you find information
   - Ⓒ lose your books

2. Library workers have to _____.
   - Ⓐ choose new books
   - Ⓑ paint the library
   - Ⓒ stay at home

3. **Information** gives you _____.
   - Ⓐ facts
   - Ⓑ questions
   - Ⓒ computers

Bonus: Draw a picture of a library. Label three things the library workers must take care of.

Maps

Introducing the Topic

1. Reproduce page 23 for individual students, or make a transparency to use with a group or your whole class.

2. Present the neighborhood map. Read and discuss all the things that are on the map. Talk about the map key, too.

Reading the Selections

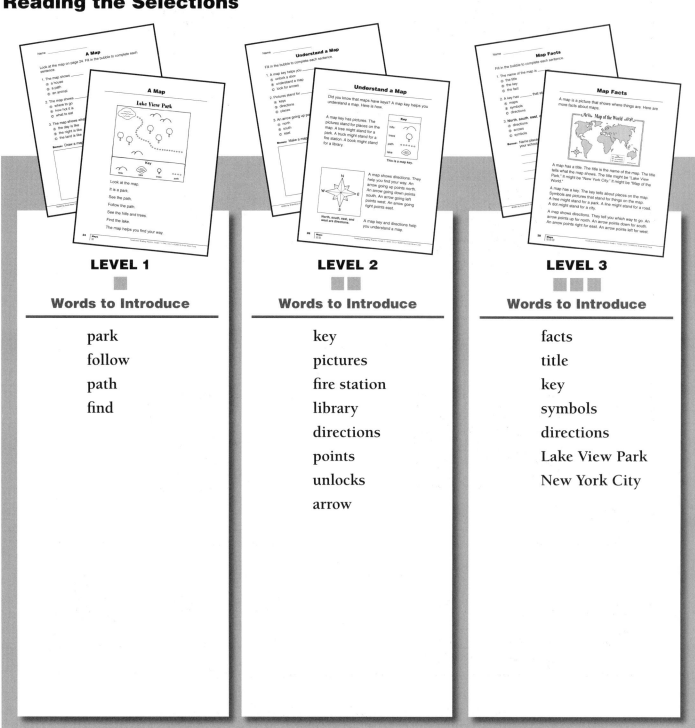

LEVEL 1	LEVEL 2	LEVEL 3
Words to Introduce	**Words to Introduce**	**Words to Introduce**
park	key	facts
follow	pictures	title
path	fire station	key
find	library	symbols
	directions	directions
	points	Lake View Park
	unlocks	New York City
	arrow	

Maria's Neighborhood

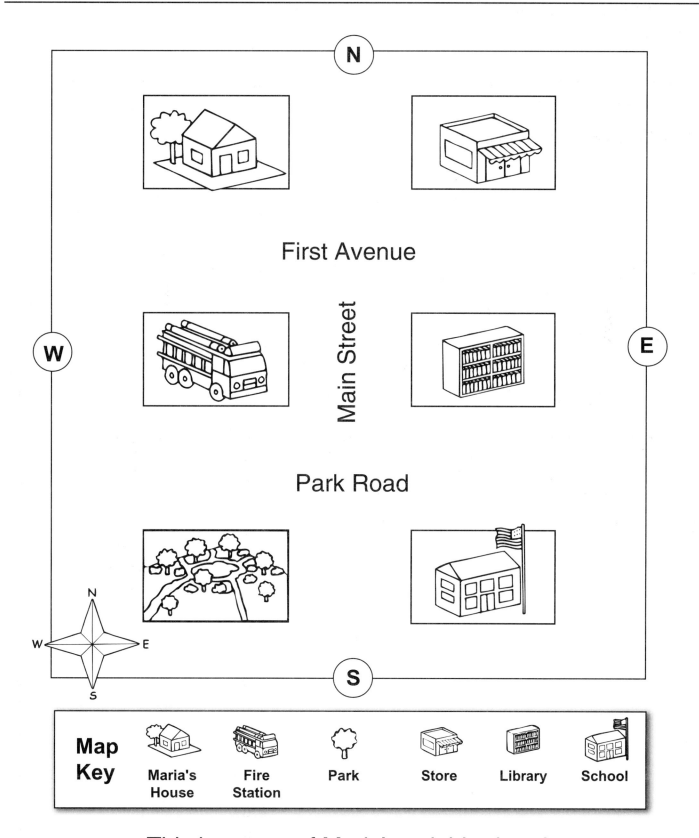

First Avenue

Main Street

Park Road

N

W   E

S

Map Key — Maria's House, Fire Station, Park, Store, Library, School

This is a map of Maria's neighborhood.

A Map

Lake View Park

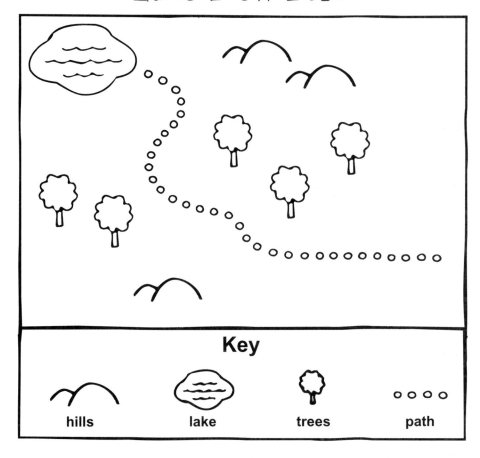

Key

| hills | lake | trees | path |

Look at the map.

It is a park.

See the path.

Follow the path.

See the hills and trees.

Find the lake.

The map helps you find your way.

Name _____

A Map

Look at the map on page 24. Fill in the bubble to complete each sentence.

1. The map shows _____.
   - Ⓐ a house
   - Ⓑ a path
   - Ⓒ an animal

2. The map shows _____.
   - Ⓐ where to go
   - Ⓑ how hot it is
   - Ⓒ what to eat

3. The map shows what _____.
   - Ⓐ the day is like
   - Ⓑ the night is like
   - Ⓒ the land is like

Bonus: Draw a map of a park you know.

Understand a Map

Did you know that maps have keys? A map key helps you understand a map. Here is how.

A map key has pictures. The pictures stand for places on the map. A tree might stand for a park. A truck might stand for a fire station. A book might stand for a library.

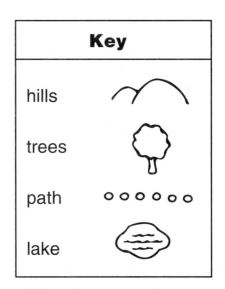

This is a map key.

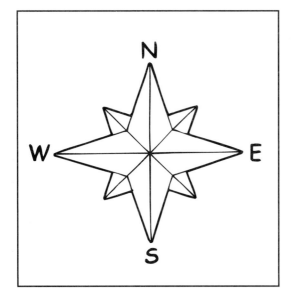

North, south, east, and west are directions.

A map shows directions. They help you find your way. An arrow going up points north. An arrow going down points south. An arrow going left points west. An arrow going right points east.

A map key and directions help you understand a map.

Nonfiction Reading Practice, Grade 1 • EMC 3312 • ©2003 by Evan-Moor Corp.

Name _____

Understand a Map

Fill in the bubble to complete each sentence.

1. A map key helps you _____.
   - Ⓐ unlock a door
   - Ⓑ understand a map
   - Ⓒ look for arrows

2. Pictures stand for _____ on a map.
   - Ⓐ keys
   - Ⓑ directions
   - Ⓒ places

3. An arrow going **up** points _____.
   - Ⓐ north
   - Ⓑ south
   - Ⓒ east

Bonus: Make a map key for your bedroom.

Map Facts

A map is a picture that shows where things are. Here are more facts about maps.

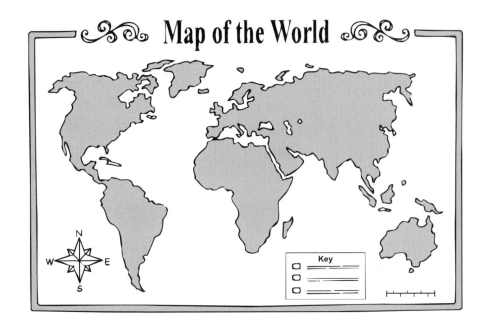

A map has a title. The title is the name of the map. The title tells what the map shows. The title might be "Lake View Park." It might be "New York City." It might be "Map of the World."

A map has a key. The key tells about places on the map. Symbols are pictures that stand for things on the map. A tree might stand for a park. A line might stand for a road. A dot might stand for a city.

A map shows directions. They tell you which way to go. An arrow points up for north. An arrow points down for south. An arrow points right for east. An arrow points left for west.

Nonfiction Reading Practice, Grade 1 • EMC 3312 • ©2003 by Evan-Moor Corp.

Name _____

Map Facts

Fill in the bubble to complete each sentence.

1. The name of the map is _____.
   - Ⓐ the title
   - Ⓑ the key
   - Ⓒ the fact

2. A key has _____ that stand for things.
   - Ⓐ maps
   - Ⓑ symbols
   - Ⓒ directions

3. **North**, **south**, **east**, and **west** are called _____.
   - Ⓐ directions
   - Ⓑ arrows
   - Ⓒ symbols

Bonus: Name places that are north, south, east, and west of your school.

_____

_____

_____

_____

Pocahontas

Introducing the Topic

1. Reproduce page 31 for individual students, or make a transparency to use with a group or your whole class.

2. Present the pictures of Pocahontas. Read and discuss the captions.

Reading the Selections

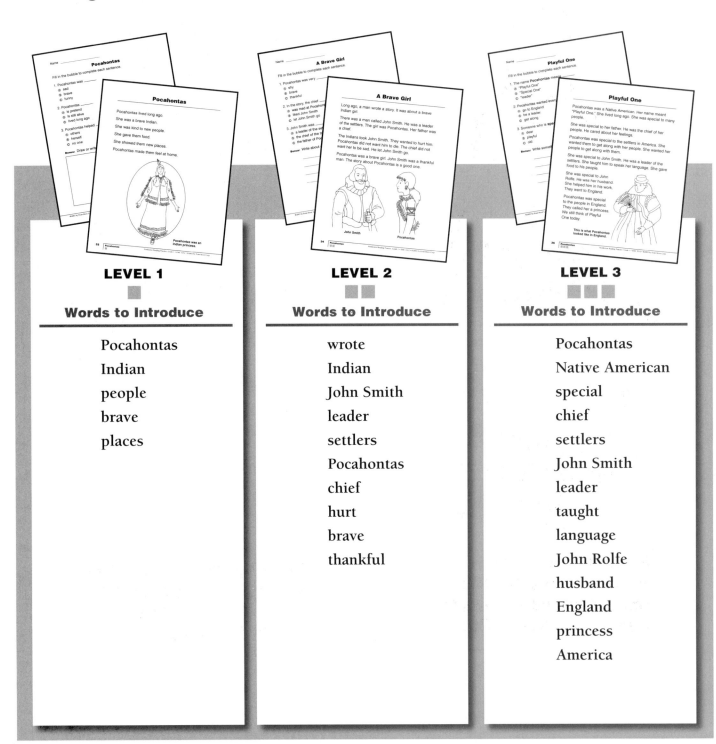

LEVEL 1

Words to Introduce

Pocahontas
Indian
people
brave
places

LEVEL 2

Words to Introduce

wrote
Indian
John Smith
leader
settlers
Pocahontas
chief
hurt
brave
thankful

LEVEL 3

Words to Introduce

Pocahontas
Native American
special
chief
settlers
John Smith
leader
taught
language
John Rolfe
husband
England
princess
America

Nonfiction Reading Practice, Grade 1 • EMC 3312 • ©2003 by Evan-Moor Corp.

Pocahontas

Playful One

Indian Princess

Pocahontas was a Powhatan Indian. Her real name was Matoaka. It means "Playful One."

The English gave her the nickname "Pocahontas." They also called her an Indian Princess.

Pocahontas

Pocahontas lived long ago.

She was a brave Indian.

She was kind to new people.

She gave them food.

She showed them new places.

Pocahontas made them feel at home.

Pocahontas was an Indian princess.

Nonfiction Reading Practice, Grade 1 • EMC 3312 • ©2003 by Evan-Moor Corp.

Name _____

Pocahontas

Fill in the bubble to complete each sentence.

1. Pocahontas was _____.
   - Ⓐ sad
   - Ⓑ brave
   - Ⓒ funny

2. Pocahontas _____.
   - Ⓐ is pretend
   - Ⓑ is still alive
   - Ⓒ lived long ago

3. Pocahontas helped _____.
   - Ⓐ others
   - Ⓑ herself
   - Ⓒ no one

Bonus: Draw or write about something brave that you did.

A Brave Girl

Long ago, a man wrote a story. It was about a brave Indian girl.

There was a man called John Smith. He was a leader of the settlers. The girl was Pocahontas. Her father was a chief.

The Indians took John Smith. They wanted to hurt him. Pocahontas did not want him to die. The chief did not want her to be sad. He let John Smith go.

Pocahontas was a brave girl. John Smith was a thankful man. The story about Pocahontas is a good one.

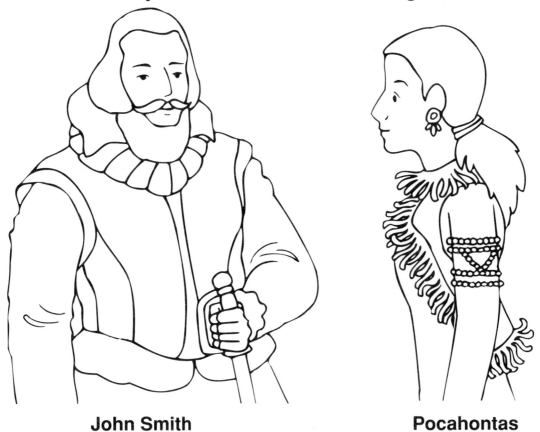

John Smith   **Pocahontas**

Name _____

A Brave Girl

Fill in the bubble to complete each sentence.

1. Pocahontas was very _____.
   - Ⓐ shy
   - Ⓑ brave
   - Ⓒ thankful

2. In the story, the chief _____.
   - Ⓐ was mad at Pocahontas
   - Ⓑ liked John Smith
   - Ⓒ let John Smith go

3. John Smith was _____.
   - Ⓐ a leader of the settlers
   - Ⓑ the chief of the tribe
   - Ⓒ the father of Pocahontas

Bonus: Write about someone who is brave.

_____

_____

_____

_____

Playful One

Pocahontas was a Native American. Her name meant "Playful One." She lived long ago. She was special to many people.

She was special to her father. He was the chief of her people. He cared about her feelings.

Pocahontas was special to the settlers in America. She wanted them to get along with her people. She wanted her people to get along with them.

She was special to John Smith. He was a leader of the settlers. She taught him to speak her language. She gave food to his people.

She was special to John Rolfe. He was her husband. She helped him in his work. They went to England.

Pocahontas was special to the people in England. They called her a princess. We still think of Playful One today.

This is what Pocahontas looked like in England.

Nonfiction Reading Practice, Grade 1 • EMC 3312 • ©2003 by Evan-Moor Corp.

Name _____

Playful One

Fill in the bubble to complete each sentence.

1. The name **Pocahontas** means _____.
   - Ⓐ "Playful One"
   - Ⓑ "Special One"
   - Ⓒ "leader"

2. Pocahontas wanted everyone to _____.
   - Ⓐ go to England
   - Ⓑ be a leader
   - Ⓒ get along

3. Someone who is **special** to you is _____.
   - Ⓐ dear
   - Ⓑ playful
   - Ⓒ old

Bonus: Write something that Pocahontas might have said.

_____

_____

_____

_____

Pyramids

Introducing the Topic

1. Reproduce page 39 for teacher use or for individual students.

2. Demonstrate the steps to make a pyramid using the pattern on page 39. Tell students that many pyramids were built in Egypt. You may also choose to have students make their own pyramid.

Reading the Selections

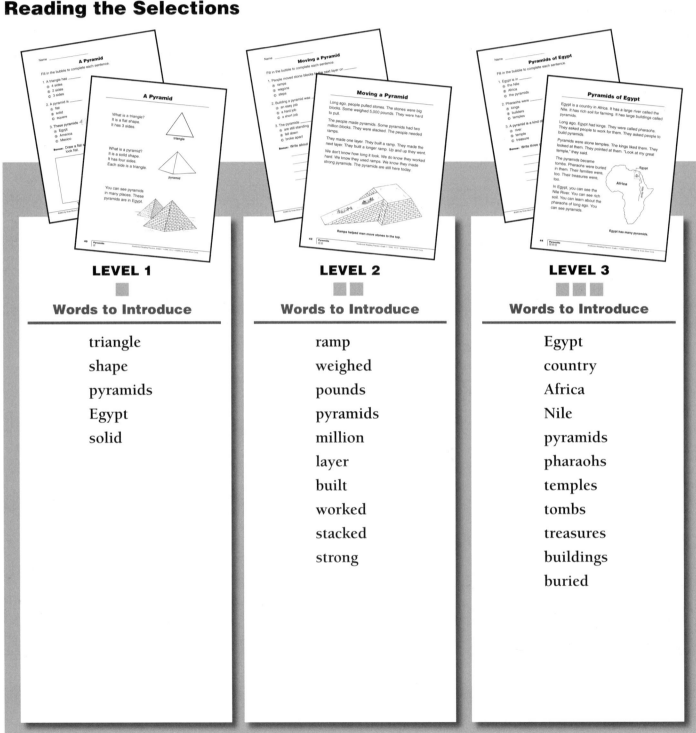

LEVEL 1

Words to Introduce

triangle

shape

pyramids

Egypt

solid

LEVEL 2

Words to Introduce

ramp

weighed

pounds

pyramids

million

layer

built

worked

stacked

strong

LEVEL 3

Words to Introduce

Egypt

country

Africa

Nile

pyramids

pharaohs

temples

tombs

treasures

buildings

buried

How to Make a Pyramid

1. Cut out the pyramid shape.
2. Fold each side of the pyramid shape.
3. Glue each folded side.
4. Now you have a pyramid.

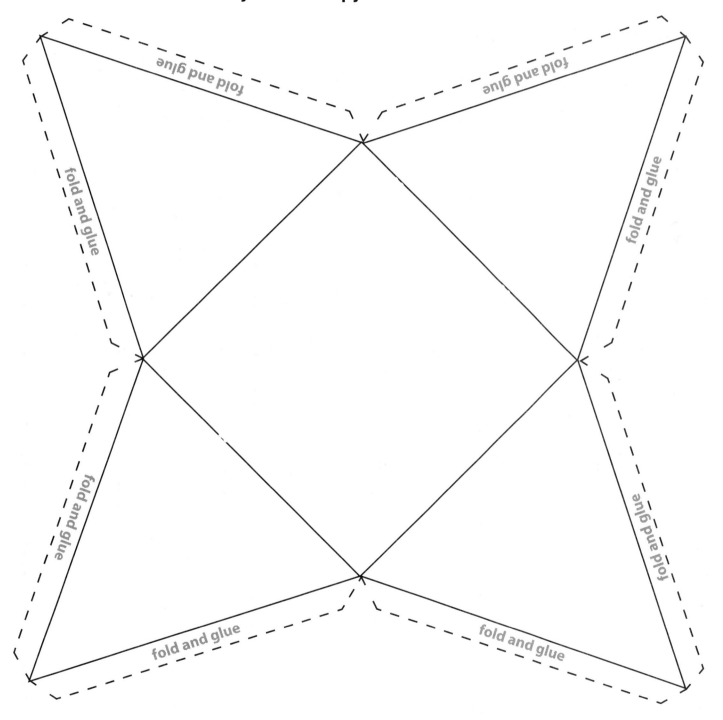

A Pyramid

What is a triangle?
It is a flat shape.
It has 3 sides.

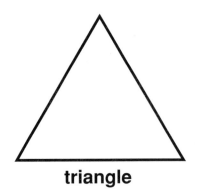

triangle

What is a pyramid?
It is a solid shape.
It has 4 sides.
Each side is a triangle.

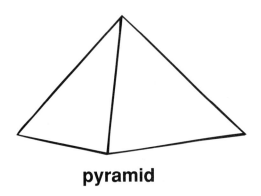

pyramid

You can see pyramids
in many places. These
pyramids are in Egypt.

Nonfiction Reading Practice, Grade 1 • EMC 3312 • ©2003 by Evan-Moor Corp.

Name _____

A Pyramid

Fill in the bubble to complete each sentence.

1. A triangle has _____.
   - Ⓐ 4 sides
   - Ⓑ 2 sides
   - Ⓒ 3 sides

2. A pyramid is _____.
   - Ⓐ flat
   - Ⓑ solid
   - Ⓒ square

3. These pyramids are in _____.
   - Ⓐ Egypt
   - Ⓑ America
   - Ⓒ Mexico

Bonus: Draw a flat shape. Then draw something that does <u>not</u> look flat.

This is flat.   This is not flat.

Moving a Pyramid

Long ago, people pulled stones. The stones were big blocks. Some weighed 5,000 pounds. They were hard to pull.

The people made pyramids. Some pyramids had two million blocks. They were stacked. The people needed ramps.

They made one layer. They built a ramp. They made the next layer. They built a longer ramp. Up and up they went.

We don't know how long it took. We do know they worked hard. We know they used ramps. We know they made strong pyramids. The pyramids are still here today.

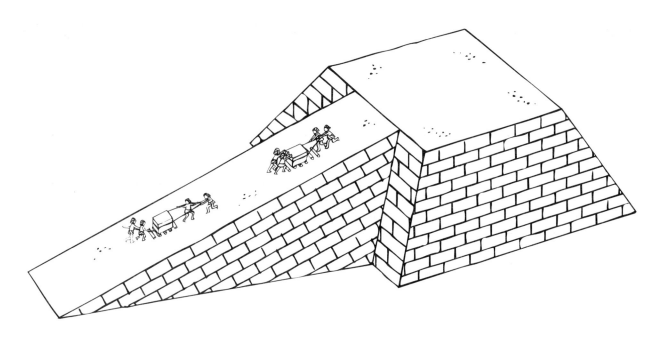

Ramps helped men move stones to the top.

Nonfiction Reading Practice, Grade 1 • EMC 3312 • ©2003 by Evan-Moor Corp.

Name _____

Moving a Pyramid

Fill in the bubble to complete each sentence.

1. People moved stone blocks to the next layer on _____.
   - Ⓐ ramps
   - Ⓑ wagons
   - Ⓒ steps

2. Building a pyramid was _____.
   - Ⓐ an easy job
   - Ⓑ a hard job
   - Ⓒ a short job

3. The pyramids _____.
   - Ⓐ are still standing
   - Ⓑ fell down
   - Ⓒ broke apart

Bonus: Write about a place where you have seen ramps being used.

_____

_____

_____

_____

Pyramids of Egypt

Egypt is a country in Africa. It has a large river called the Nile. It has rich soil for farming. It has large buildings called pyramids.

Long ago, Egypt had kings. They were called pharaohs. They asked people to work for them. They asked people to build pyramids.

Pyramids were stone temples. The kings liked them. They looked at them. They pointed at them. "Look at my great temple," they said.

The pyramids became tombs. Pharaohs were buried in them. Their families were, too. Their treasures were, too.

In Egypt, you can see the Nile River. You can see rich soil. You can learn about the pharaohs of long ago. You can see pyramids.

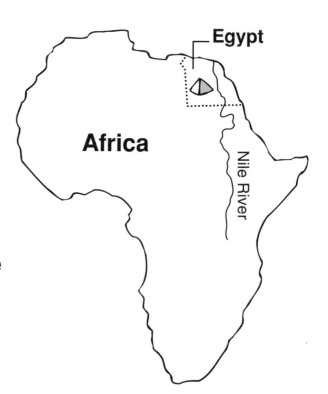

Egypt has many pyramids.

Nonfiction Reading Practice, Grade 1 • EMC 3312 • ©2003 by Evan-Moor Corp.

Name _____

Pyramids of Egypt

Fill in the bubble to complete each sentence.

1. Egypt is in _____.
   - Ⓐ the Nile
   - Ⓑ Africa
   - Ⓒ the pyramids

2. **Pharaohs** were _____.
   - Ⓐ kings
   - Ⓑ builders
   - Ⓒ temples

3. A pyramid is a kind of _____.
   - Ⓐ river
   - Ⓑ temple
   - Ⓒ treasure

Bonus: Write three questions you would ask if you could visit Egypt.

_____

_____

_____

_____

Animal Habitats

Introducing the Topic

1. Reproduce page 47 for individual students, or make a transparency to use with a group or your whole class.

2. Present the chart about animals and their homes. Read and discuss the different kinds of habitats.

Reading the Selections

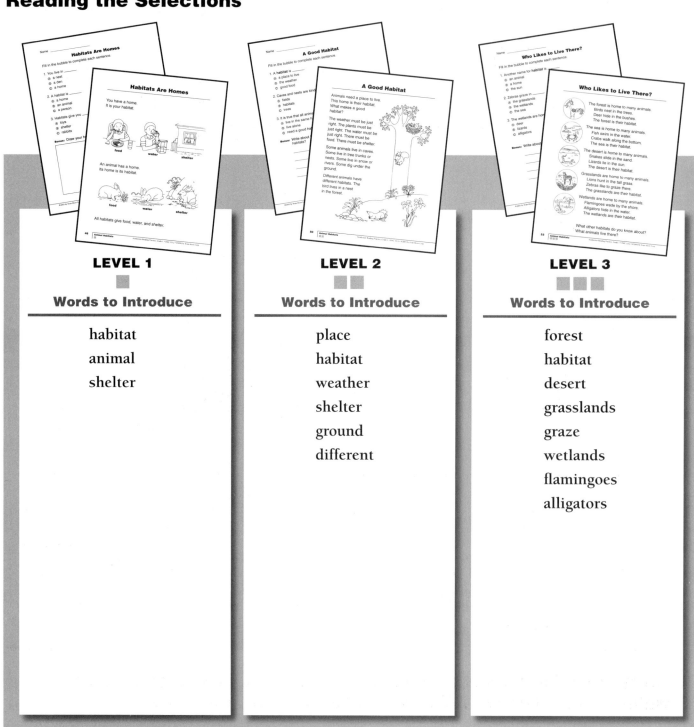

LEVEL 1	LEVEL 2	LEVEL 3
Words to Introduce	**Words to Introduce**	**Words to Introduce**
habitat	place	forest
animal	habitat	habitat
shelter	weather	desert
	shelter	grasslands
	ground	graze
	different	wetlands
		flamingoes
		alligators

Nonfiction Reading Practice, Grade 1 • EMC 3312 • ©2003 by Evan-Moor Corp.

Animal Habitats

Animal	Home
 elephant	grasslands
bee	hive
bird	nest
dolphin	ocean

Every animal has a special home, or habitat. The habitat gives food, water, and shelter. Which of these habitats have you seen?

Habitats Are Homes

You have a home.
It is your habitat.

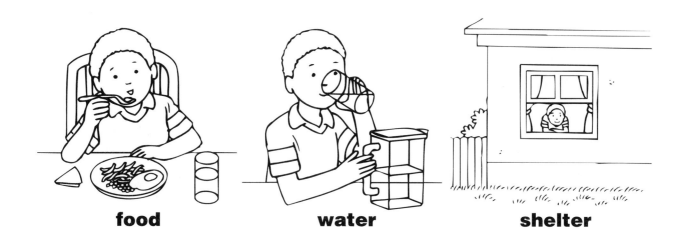

food

water

shelter

An animal has a home.
Its home is its habitat.

food

water

shelter

All habitats give food, water, and shelter.

Nonfiction Reading Practice, Grade 1 • EMC 3312 • ©2003 by Evan-Moor Corp.

Name _____

Habitats Are Homes

Fill in the bubble to complete each sentence.

1. You live in _____.
   - Ⓐ a nest
   - Ⓑ a den
   - Ⓒ a home

2. A **habitat** is _____.
   - Ⓐ a home
   - Ⓑ an animal
   - Ⓒ a person

3. Habitats give you _____.
   - Ⓐ toys
   - Ⓑ shelter
   - Ⓒ rabbits

Bonus: Draw your habitat.

A Good Habitat

Animals need a place to live.
This home is their habitat.
What makes a good
habitat?

The weather must be just
right. The plants must be
just right. The water must be
just right. There must be
food. There must be shelter.

Some animals live in caves.
Some live in tree trunks or
nests. Some live in snow or
rivers. Some dig under the
ground.

Different animals have
different habitats.

Name _____

A Good Habitat

Fill in the bubble to complete each sentence.

1. A **habitat** is _____.
   - Ⓐ a place to live
   - Ⓑ the weather
   - Ⓒ good food

2. Caves and nests are kinds of _____.
   - Ⓐ fields
   - Ⓑ habitats
   - Ⓒ trees

3. It is true that all animals _____.
   - Ⓐ live in the same habitat
   - Ⓑ live alone
   - Ⓒ need a good habitat

Bonus: Write about two animals that live near you. What are their habitats?

_____

_____

_____

_____

Who Likes to Live There?

The **forest** is home to many animals.
    Birds nest in the trees.
    Deer hide in the bushes.
    The forest is their habitat.

The **sea** is home to many animals.
    Fish swim in the water.
    Crabs walk along the bottom.
    The sea is their habitat.

The **desert** is home to many animals.
    Snakes slide in the sand.
    Lizards lie in the sun.
    The desert is their habitat.

Grasslands are home to many animals.
    Lions hunt in the tall grass.
    Zebras like to graze there.
    The grasslands are their habitat.

Wetlands are home to many animals.
    Flamingoes wade by the shore.
    Alligators hide in the water.
    The wetlands are their habitat.

What other habitats do you know about?
What animals live there?

Name _____

Who Likes to Live There?

Fill in the bubble to complete each sentence.

1. Another name for **habitat** is _____.
   - Ⓐ an animal
   - Ⓑ a home
   - Ⓒ the sun

2. Zebras graze in _____.
   - Ⓐ the grasslands
   - Ⓑ the wetlands
   - Ⓒ the sea

3. The wetlands are home to flamingoes and _____.
   - Ⓐ deer
   - Ⓑ lizards
   - Ⓒ alligators

Bonus: Write about a habitat you would like to visit. Why?

_____

_____

_____

_____

Matter

Introducing the Topic

1. Reproduce page 55 for individual students, or make a transparency to use with a group or your whole class.

2. Present the solid/liquid/gas properties chart. Read and discuss the three kinds of matter. Name other examples of solids, liquids, and gases.

Reading the Selections

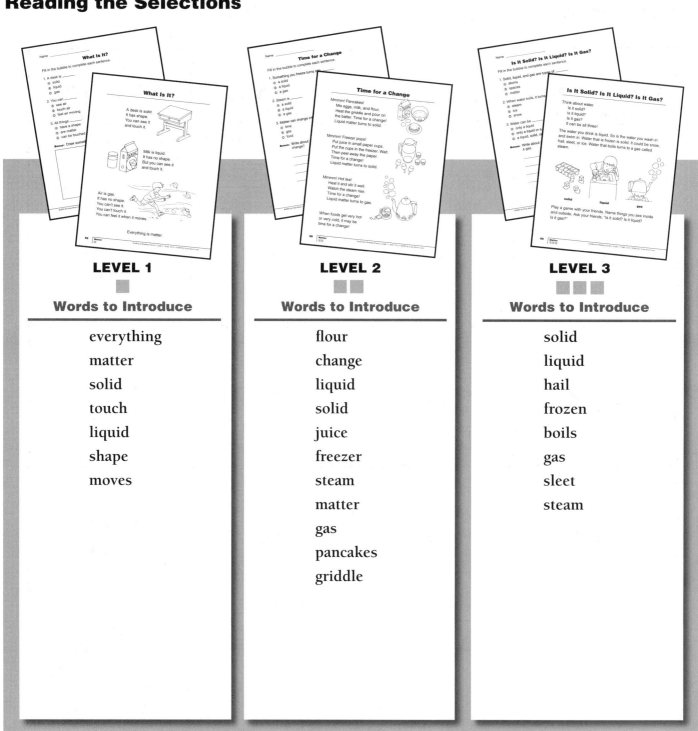

LEVEL 1

Words to Introduce

everything

matter

solid

touch

liquid

shape

moves

LEVEL 2

Words to Introduce

flour

change

liquid

solid

juice

freezer

steam

matter

gas

pancakes

griddle

LEVEL 3

Words to Introduce

solid

liquid

hail

frozen

boils

gas

sleet

steam

Matter

Solids, liquids, and gases
are kinds of matter.

How are they alike?
How are they different?

What is one type of matter?	Does it have a shape?	Can you see it and touch it?	What are some examples?
Solid	yes	yes	chair, leaf
Liquid	no	yes	water, syrup
Gas	no	no	steam, helium

What Is It?

A desk is solid.
It has shape.
You can see it
and touch it.

Milk is liquid.
It has no shape.
But you can see it
and touch it.

Air is gas.
It has no shape.
You can't see it.
You can't touch it.
You can feel it when it moves.

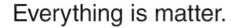

Everything is matter.

Nonfiction Reading Practice, Grade 1 • EMC 3312 • ©2003 by Evan-Moor Corp.

Name _____

What Is It?

Fill in the bubble to complete each sentence.

1. A desk is _____.
   - Ⓐ solid
   - Ⓑ liquid
   - Ⓒ gas

2. You can _____.
   - Ⓐ see air
   - Ⓑ touch air
   - Ⓒ feel air moving

3. All things _____.
   - Ⓐ have a shape
   - Ⓑ are matter
   - Ⓒ can be touched

Bonus: Draw something solid. Is it matter? _____

Time for a Change

Mmmm! Pancakes!
    Mix eggs, milk, and flour.
    Heat the griddle and pour on
    the batter. Time for a change!
    Liquid matter turns to solid.

Mmmm! Freezer pops!
    Put juice in small paper cups.
    Put the cups in the freezer. Wait.
    Then peel away the paper.
    Time for a change!
    Liquid matter turns to solid.

Mmmm! Hot tea!
    Heat it and stir it well.
    Watch the steam rise.
    Time for a change!
    Liquid matter turns to gas.

When foods get very hot
or very cold, it may be
time for a change!

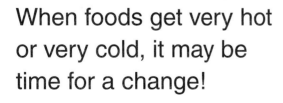

Nonfiction Reading Practice, Grade 1 • EMC 3312 • ©2003 by Evan-Moor Corp.

Name _____

Time for a Change

Fill in the bubble to complete each sentence.

1. Something you freeze turns into _____.
   Ⓐ a solid
   Ⓑ a liquid
   Ⓒ a gas

2. **Steam** is _____.
   Ⓐ a solid
   Ⓑ a liquid
   Ⓒ a gas

3. Matter can change into a liquid, solid, or _____.
   Ⓐ time
   Ⓑ gas
   Ⓒ food

Bonus: Write about a food you have helped prepare. How did it change?

_____

_____

_____

_____

Is It Solid? Is It Liquid? Is It Gas?

Think about water.
　　Is it solid?
　　Is it liquid?
　　Is it gas?
　　It can be all three!

The water you drink is liquid. So is the water you wash in and swim in. Water that is frozen is solid. It could be snow, hail, sleet, or ice. Water that boils turns into a gas called steam.

solid　　　　　　**liquid**　　　　　　**gas**

Play a game with your friends. Name things you see inside and outside. Ask your friends, "Is it solid? Is it liquid? Is it gas?"

Name _____

Is It Solid? Is It Liquid? Is It Gas?

Fill in the bubble to complete each sentence.

1. **Solid**, **liquid**, and **gas** are types of _____.
   - Ⓐ atoms
   - Ⓑ spaces
   - Ⓒ matter

2. When water boils, it turns into _____.
   - Ⓐ steam
   - Ⓑ ice
   - Ⓒ snow

3. Water can be _____.
   - Ⓐ only a liquid
   - Ⓑ only a liquid or a gas
   - Ⓒ a liquid, solid, or gas

Bonus: Write about ways you use water as a liquid, a solid, and a gas.

_____

_____

_____

_____

Neil Armstrong

Introducing the Topic

1. Reproduce page 63 for individual students, or make a transparency to use with a group or your whole class.

2. Present the time line. Read and discuss the fact that Neil Armstrong is a famous astronaut who was the first person to land on the moon.

Reading the Selections

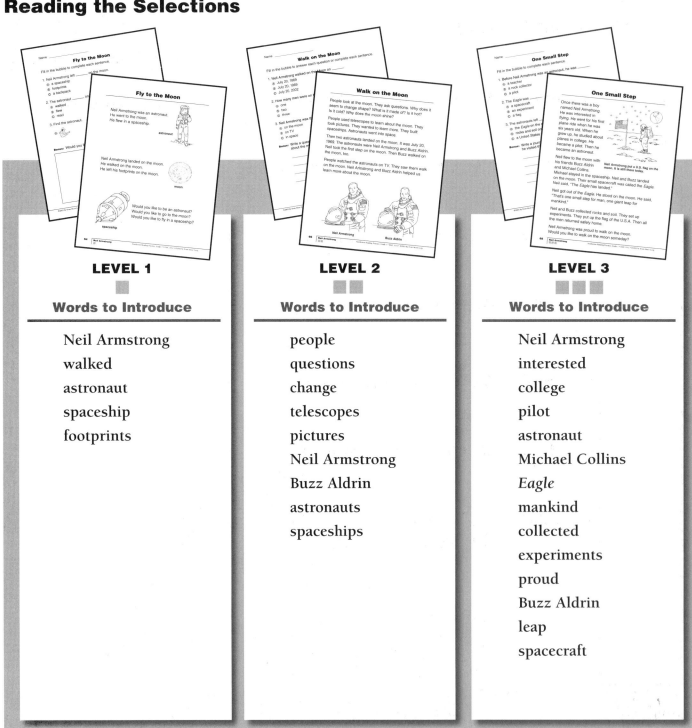

LEVEL 1

Words to Introduce

Neil Armstrong

walked

astronaut

spaceship

footprints

LEVEL 2

Words to Introduce

people

questions

change

telescopes

pictures

Neil Armstrong

Buzz Aldrin

astronauts

spaceships

LEVEL 3

Words to Introduce

Neil Armstrong

interested

college

pilot

astronaut

Michael Collins

Eagle

mankind

collected

experiments

proud

Buzz Aldrin

leap

spacecraft

Time Line of Neil Armstrong

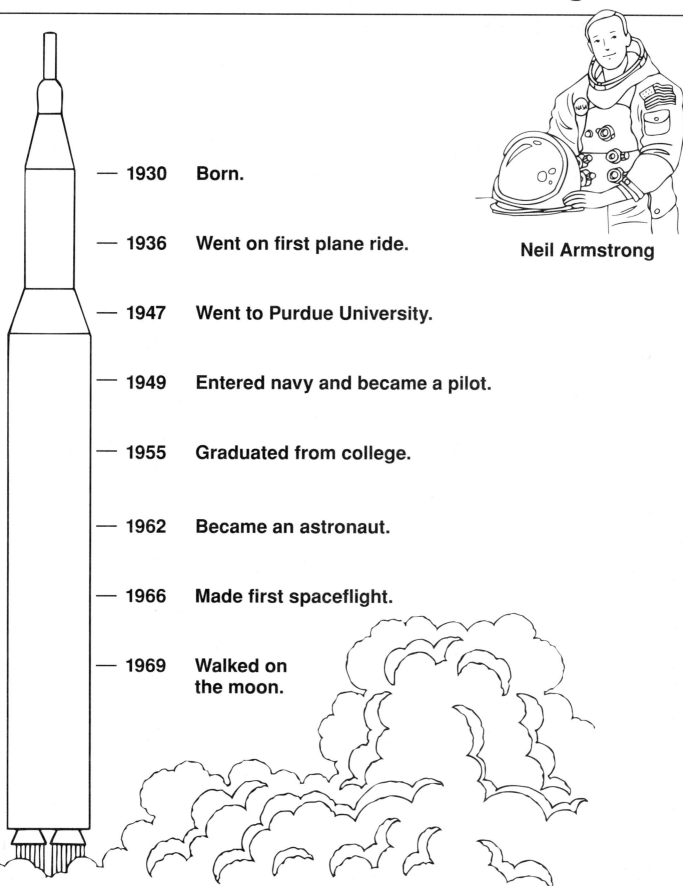

Neil Armstrong

— 1930   **Born.**

— 1936   **Went on first plane ride.**

— 1947   **Went to Purdue University.**

— 1949   **Entered navy and became a pilot.**

— 1955   **Graduated from college.**

— 1962   **Became an astronaut.**

— 1966   **Made first spaceflight.**

— 1969   **Walked on the moon.**

Fly to the Moon

Neil Armstrong was an astronaut.
He went to the moon.
He flew in a spaceship.

astronaut

Neil Armstrong landed on the moon.
He walked on the moon.
He left his footprints on the moon.

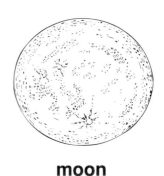

moon

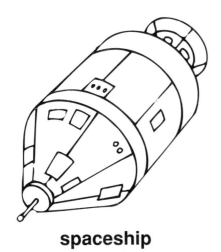

spaceship

Would you like to be an astronaut?
Would you like to go to the moon?
Would you like to fly in a spaceship?

Name _____

Fly to the Moon

Fill in the bubble to answe r each question or complete each sentence.

1. Neil Armstrong left _____ on the moon.
   - Ⓐ a spaceship
   - Ⓑ footprints
   - Ⓒ a backpack

2. The astronaut _____ on the moon.
   - Ⓐ walked
   - Ⓑ flew
   - Ⓒ read

3. Find the astronaut.

Ⓐ    Ⓑ    Ⓒ

Bonus: Would you like to go to the moon? Draw or write why.

Walk on the Moon

People look at the moon. They ask questions. Why does it seem to change shape? What is it made of? Is it hot? Is it cold? Why does the moon shine?

People used telescopes to learn about the moon. They took pictures. They wanted to learn more. They built spaceships. Astronauts went into space.

Then two astronauts landed on the moon. It was July 20, 1969. The astronauts were Neil Armstrong and Buzz Aldrin. Neil took the first step on the moon. Then Buzz walked on the moon, too.

People watched the astronauts on TV. They saw them walk on the moon. Neil Armstrong and Buzz Aldrin helped us learn more about the moon.

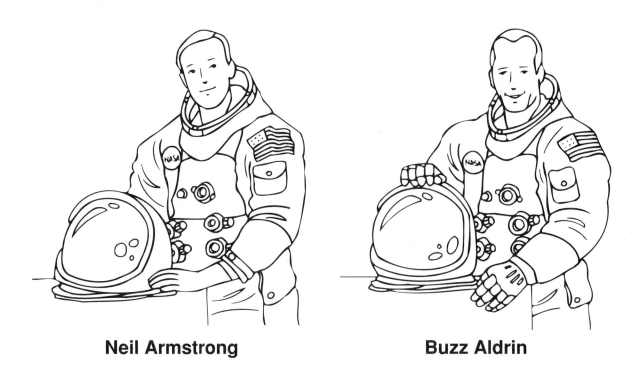

Neil Armstrong   **Buzz Aldrin**

Nonfiction Reading Practice, Grade 1 • EMC 3312 • ©2003 by Evan-Moor Corp.

Name _____

Walk on the Moon

Fill in the bubble to answer each question or complete each sentence.

1. Neil Armstrong walked on the moon on _____.
   - Ⓐ July 20, 1869
   - Ⓑ July 20, 1969
   - Ⓒ July 20, 2002

2. How many men were on the moon?
   - Ⓐ one
   - Ⓑ two
   - Ⓒ three

3. Neil Armstrong was the first astronaut _____.
   - Ⓐ on the moon
   - Ⓑ on TV
   - Ⓒ in space

Bonus: Write a question you would like to ask Neil Armstrong about the moon.

_____

_____

_____

_____

One Small Step

Once there was a boy named Neil Armstrong. He was interested in flying. He went for his first plane ride when he was six years old. When he grew up, he studied about planes in college. He became a pilot. Then he became an astronaut.

Neil Armstrong put a U.S. flag on the moon. It is still there today.

Neil flew to the moon with his friends Buzz Aldrin and Michael Collins. Their small spacecraft was called the *Eagle*. Neil said, "The *Eagle* has landed."

Neil got out of the *Eagle*. He stood on the moon. He said, "That's one small step for man, one giant leap for mankind."

Neil and Buzz collected rocks and soil. They set up experiments. They put up the flag of the U.S.A. Then all the men returned safely home.

Neil Armstrong was proud to walk on the moon. Would you like to walk on the moon someday?

Nonfiction Reading Practice, Grade 1 • EMC 3312 • ©2003 by Evan-Moor Corp.

Name _____

One Small Step

Fill in the bubble to complete each sentence.

1. Before Neil Armstrong was an astronaut, he was _____.
   - Ⓐ a teacher
   - Ⓑ a rock collector
   - Ⓒ a pilot

2. The *Eagle* was _____.
   - Ⓐ a spacecraft
   - Ⓑ an experiment
   - Ⓒ a flag

3. The astronauts left _____.
   - Ⓐ the *Eagle* on the moon
   - Ⓑ rocks and soil on the moon
   - Ⓒ a United States flag on the moon

Bonus: Write a journal entry Neil Armstrong might have made when he visited the moon.

_____

_____

_____

_____

Thermometers

Introducing the Topic

1. Reproduce page 71 for individual students, or make a transparency to use with a group or your whole class.

2. Present the pictures of thermometers. Read and discuss the labels.

Reading the Selections

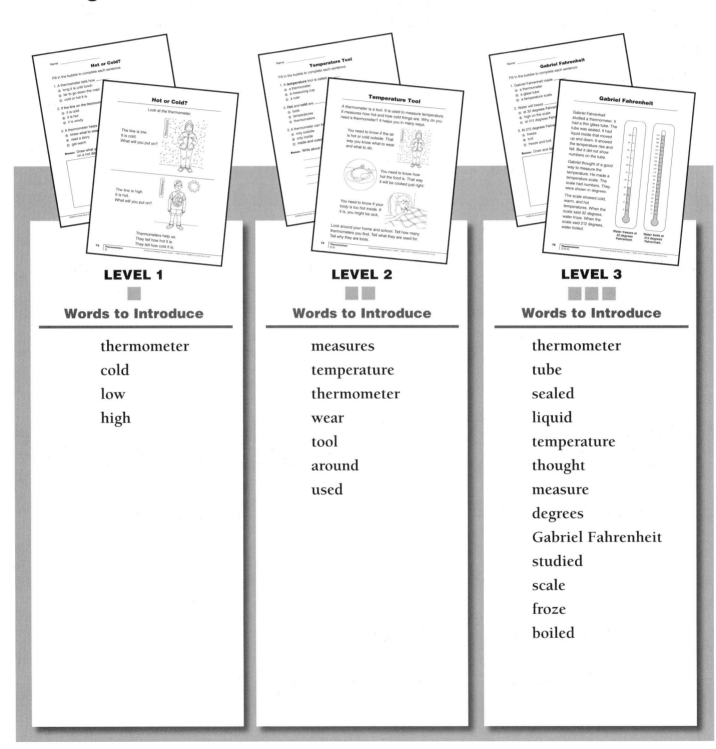

LEVEL 1

Words to Introduce

thermometer

cold

low

high

LEVEL 2

Words to Introduce

measures

temperature

thermometer

wear

tool

around

used

LEVEL 3

Words to Introduce

thermometer

tube

sealed

liquid

temperature

thought

measure

degrees

Gabriel Fahrenheit

studied

scale

froze

boiled

Nonfiction Reading Practice, Grade 1 • EMC 3312 • ©2003 by Evan-Moor Corp.

Using a Thermometer

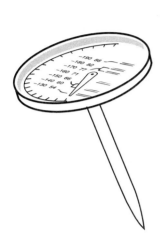

Meat Thermometer

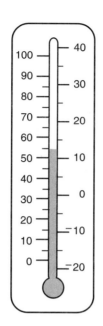

Wall Thermometer

Outdoor Thermometer

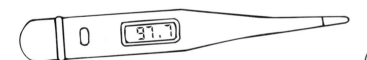

Digital Thermometer

Oral Thermometer

We use the thermometer.

The thermometer measures how hot or cold it is.

Hot or Cold?

Look at the thermometer.

The line is low.
It is cold.
What will you put on?

The line is high.
It is hot.
What will you put on?

Thermometers help us.
They tell how hot it is.
They tell how cold it is.

Nonfiction Reading Practice, Grade 1 • EMC 3312 • ©2003 by Evan-Moor Corp.

Name _____

Hot or Cold?

Fill in the bubble to complete each sentence.

1. A thermometer tells how _____.
   - Ⓐ long it is until lunch
   - Ⓑ far to go down the road
   - Ⓒ cold or hot it is

2. If the line on the thermometer is high, it is _____.
   - Ⓐ cold
   - Ⓑ hot
   - Ⓒ windy

3. A thermometer helps you _____.
   - Ⓐ know what to wear
   - Ⓑ read a story
   - Ⓒ get warm

Bonus: Draw what you wear on a hot day. Draw what you wear on a cold day.

It is hot.	It is cold.

Temperature Tool

A thermometer is a tool. It is used to measure temperature. It measures how hot and how cold things are. Why do you need a thermometer? It helps you in many ways.

You need to know if the air is hot or cold outside. That way you know what to wear and what to do.

You need to know how hot the food is. That way it will be cooked just right.

You need to know if your body is too hot inside. If it is, you might be sick.

Look around your home and school. Tell how many thermometers you find. Tell what they are used for. Tell why they are tools.

Nonfiction Reading Practice, Grade 1 • EMC 3312 • ©2003 by Evan-Moor Corp.

Name _____

Temperature Tool

Fill in the bubble to complete each sentence.

1. A **temperature tool** is called _____.
   - Ⓐ a thermometer
   - Ⓑ a measuring cup
   - Ⓒ a ruler

2. **Hot** and **cold** are _____.
   - Ⓐ tools
   - Ⓑ temperatures
   - Ⓒ thermometers

3. A thermometer can be used _____.
   - Ⓐ only outside
   - Ⓑ only inside
   - Ⓒ inside and outside

Bonus: Write about ways you use a thermometer.

_____

_____

_____

_____

Gabriel Fahrenheit

Gabriel Fahrenheit studied a thermometer. It had a thin glass tube. The tube was sealed. It had liquid inside that moved up and down. It showed the temperature rise and fall. But it did not show numbers on the tube.

Gabriel thought of a good way to measure the temperature. He made a temperature scale. The scale had numbers. They were shown in degrees.

The scale showed cold, warm, and hot temperatures. When the scale said 32 degrees, water froze. When the scale said 212 degrees, water boiled.

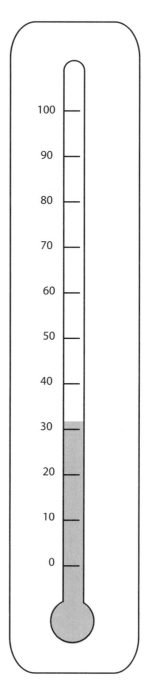

Water freezes at 32 degrees Fahrenheit.

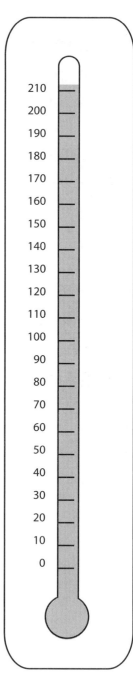

Water boils at 212 degrees Fahrenheit.

Name _____

Gabriel Fahrenheit

Fill in the bubble to complete each sentence.

1. Gabriel Fahrenheit made _____.
   - Ⓐ a thermometer
   - Ⓑ a glass tube
   - Ⓒ a temperature scale

2. Water will freeze _____.
   - Ⓐ at 32 degrees Fahrenheit
   - Ⓑ high on the scale
   - Ⓒ at 212 degrees Fahrenheit

3. At 212 degrees Fahrenheit, water will _____.
   - Ⓐ freeze
   - Ⓑ boil
   - Ⓒ freeze and boil

Bonus: Draw and label something else that has a measurement scale.

The Sun

Introducing the Topic

1. Reproduce page 79 for individual students, or make a transparency to use with a group or your whole class.

2. Present the diagram of the solar system. Show students that the sun is in the center. Discuss why people and plants need the sun on Earth.

Reading the Selections

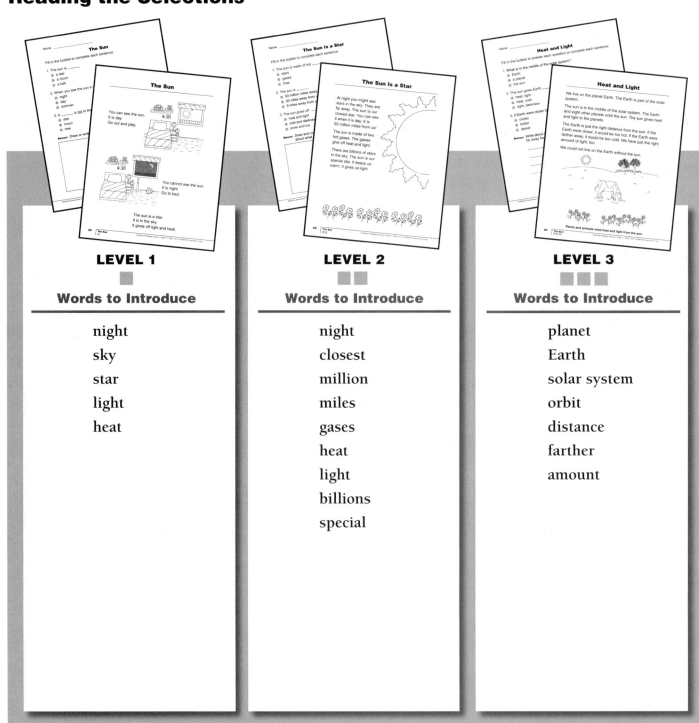

LEVEL 1	LEVEL 2	LEVEL 3
■	■ ■	■ ■ ■
Words to Introduce	**Words to Introduce**	**Words to Introduce**
night	night	planet
sky	closest	Earth
star	million	solar system
light	miles	orbit
heat	gases	distance
	heat	farther
	light	amount
	billions	
	special	

The Sun

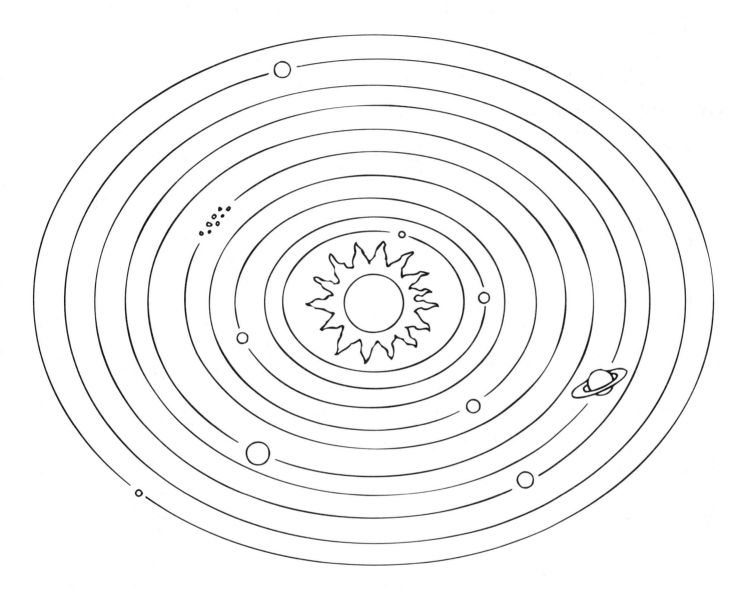

This is the solar system. The planets orbit the sun.

The Sun

You can see the sun.
It is day.
Go out and play.

You cannot see the sun.
It is night.
Go to bed.

The sun is a star.
It is in the sky.
It gives off light and heat.

Name _____

The Sun

Fill in the bubble to complete each sentence.

1. The sun is _____.
   - Ⓐ a star
   - Ⓑ a moon
   - Ⓒ a ball

2. When you see the sun in the sky, it is _____.
   - Ⓐ night
   - Ⓑ day
   - Ⓒ summer

3. A _____ is <u>not</u> in the sky.
   - Ⓐ star
   - Ⓑ moon
   - Ⓒ tree

Bonus: Draw or write about what you like to do on a sunny day.

The Sun Is a Star

At night you might see stars in the sky. They are far away. The sun is our closest star. You can see it when it is day. It is 93 million miles from us!

The sun is made of two hot gases. The gases give off heat and light.

There are billions of stars in the sky. The sun is our special star. It keeps us warm. It gives us light.

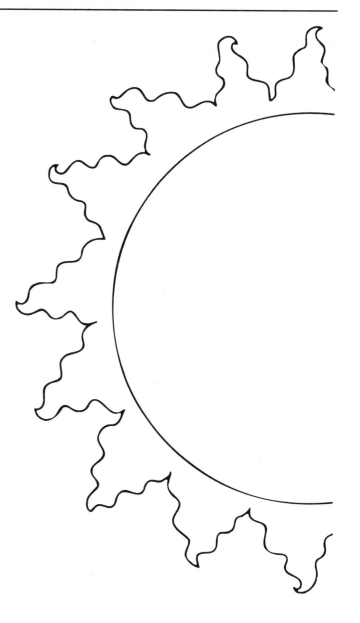

Nonfiction Reading Practice, Grade 1 • EMC 3312 • ©2003 by Evan-Moor Corp.

Name _____

The Sun Is a Star

Fill in the bubble to complete each sentence.

1. The sun is made of hot _____.
   - Ⓐ stars
   - Ⓑ gases
   - Ⓒ fires

2. The sun is _____ away from us.
   - Ⓐ 93 million miles
   - Ⓑ 93 miles
   - Ⓒ 9 miles

3. The sun gives off _____.
   - Ⓐ heat and light
   - Ⓑ cold and darkness
   - Ⓒ snow and ice

Bonus: Draw and color a picture of the hot sun. Write a sentence about what you learned about the sun.

Heat and Light

We live on the planet Earth. The Earth is part of the solar system.

The sun is in the middle of the solar system. The Earth and eight other planets orbit the sun. The sun gives heat and light to the planets.

The Earth is just the right distance from the sun. If the Earth were closer, it would be too hot. If the Earth were farther away, it would be too cold. We have just the right amount of light, too.

We could not live on the Earth without the sun.

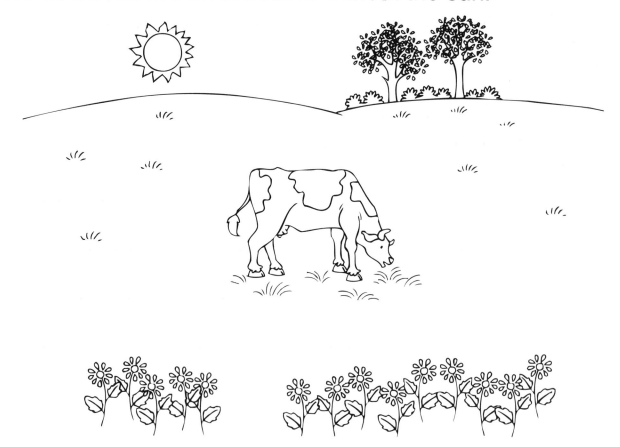

Plants and animals need heat and light from the sun.

Name _____

Heat and Light

Fill in the bubble to answer each question or complete each sentence.

1. What is in the middle of the solar system?
   - Ⓐ Earth
   - Ⓑ a planet
   - Ⓒ the sun

2. The sun gives Earth _____ and _____.
   - Ⓐ heat, light
   - Ⓑ heat, cold
   - Ⓒ light, darkness

3. If Earth were closer to the sun, Earth would be _____.
   - Ⓐ colder
   - Ⓑ hotter
   - Ⓒ darker

Bonus: Write about what it might be like on another planet that is far away from the sun.

_____

_____

_____

_____

Bike Helmets

Introducing the Topic

1. Reproduce page 87 for individual students, or make a transparency to use with a group or your whole class.

2. Present the diagram showing the correct and incorrect ways to wear a bike helmet. Read and discuss the captions.

Reading the Selections

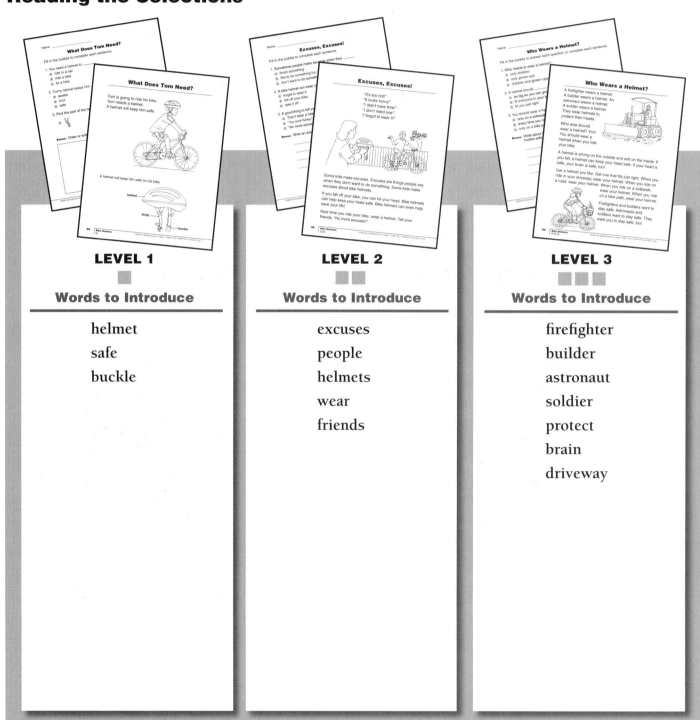

LEVEL 1	LEVEL 2	LEVEL 3
■	■ ■	■ ■ ■
Words to Introduce	**Words to Introduce**	**Words to Introduce**
helmet	excuses	firefighter
safe	people	builder
buckle	helmets	astronaut
	wear	soldier
	friends	protect
		brain
		driveway

Nonfiction Reading Practice, Grade 1 • EMC 3312 • ©2003 by Evan-Moor Corp.

Bike Helmets

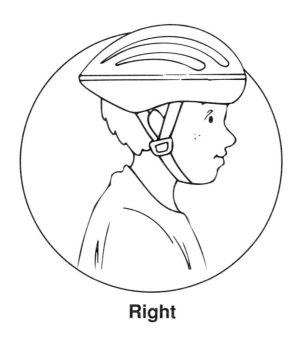

Right

A bike helmet should not tilt forward
or backward on your head.

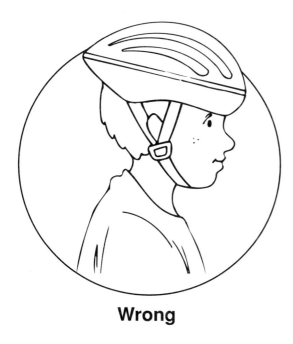

Wrong

Wrong

What Does Tom Need?

Tom is going to ride his bike.
Tom needs a helmet.
A helmet will keep him safe.

A helmet will keep him safe on his bike.

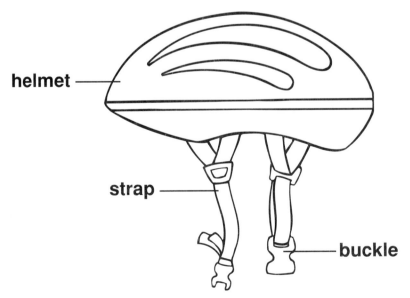

helmet

strap

buckle

Nonfiction Reading Practice, Grade 1 • EMC 3312 • ©2003 by Evan-Moor Corp.

Name _____

What Does Tom Need?

Fill in the bubble to answer each question or complete each sentence.

1. You need a helmet to _____.
   - Ⓐ ride in a car
   - Ⓑ ride a bike
   - Ⓒ fix a bike

2. Tom's helmet keeps him _____.
   - Ⓐ awake
   - Ⓑ cool
   - Ⓒ safe

3. Find the part of the helmet that goes under your chin.

   Ⓐ   Ⓑ    Ⓒ

Bonus: Draw or write about how you keep safe when you play.

Excuses, Excuses!

"It's too hot!"

"It looks funny!"

"I didn't have time!"

"I don't need one!"

"I forgot to wear it!"

Some kids make excuses. Excuses are things people say when they don't want to do something. Some kids make excuses about bike helmets.

If you fall off your bike, you can hit your head. Bike helmets can help keep your head safe. Bike helmets can even help save your life!

Next time you ride your bike, wear a helmet. Tell your friends, "No more excuses!"

Name _____

Excuses, Excuses!

Fill in the bubble to complete each sentence.

1. Sometimes people make excuses when they _____.
   - Ⓐ finish something
   - Ⓑ like to do something fun
   - Ⓒ don't want to do something

2. A bike helmet can keep you safe if you _____.
   - Ⓐ forget to wear it
   - Ⓑ fall off your bike
   - Ⓒ take it off

3. A good thing to tell your friends is, _____.
   - Ⓐ "Don't wear a helmet."
   - Ⓑ "You look funny."
   - Ⓒ "No more excuses!"

Bonus: Write an excuse you have heard someone say.

_____

_____

_____

_____

Who Wears a Helmet?

A firefighter wears a helmet.
A builder wears a helmet. An
astronaut wears a helmet.
A soldier wears a helmet.
They wear helmets to
protect their heads.

Who else should
wear a helmet? You!
You should wear a
helmet when you ride
your bike.

A helmet is strong on the outside and soft on the inside.
If you fall, a helmet can keep your head safe. If your head
is safe, your brain is safe, too!

Get a helmet you like. Get one that fits just right. When you
ride on your driveway, wear your helmet. When you ride on
a road, wear your helmet. When you ride on a bike path,
wear your helmet.

Firefighters and builders want
to stay safe. Astronauts and
soldiers want to stay safe.
They want you to stay safe, too!

Name _____

Who Wears a Helmet?

Fill in the bubble to answer each question or complete each sentence.

1. Who needs to wear a helmet?
   - Ⓐ only children
   - Ⓑ only grown-ups
   - Ⓒ children and grown-ups

2. A helmet should _____.
   - Ⓐ be big so you can grow into it
   - Ⓑ fit everyone in your family
   - Ⓒ fit you just right

3. You should wear a helmet _____.
   - Ⓐ only on a road
   - Ⓑ every time you ride your bike
   - Ⓒ only on a bike path

Bonus: Write about things people wear to keep other parts of their bodies safe.

_____

_____

_____

_____

Dr. Jonas Salk

Introducing the Topic

1. Reproduce page 95 for individual students, or make a transparency to use with a group or your whole class.

2. Present the pictures, emphasizing that a new vaccine was invented by Jonas Salk. Tell students that a vaccine is a medicine that prevents an illness.

Reading the Selections

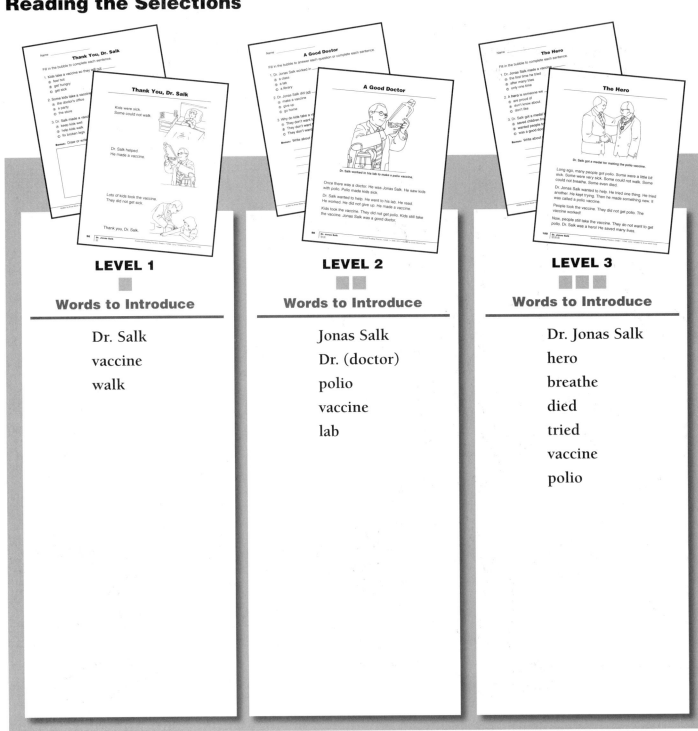

LEVEL 1

Words to Introduce

Dr. Salk

vaccine

walk

LEVEL 2

Words to Introduce

Jonas Salk

Dr. (doctor)

polio

vaccine

lab

LEVEL 3

Words to Introduce

Dr. Jonas Salk

hero

breathe

died

tried

vaccine

polio

Dr. Jonas Salk

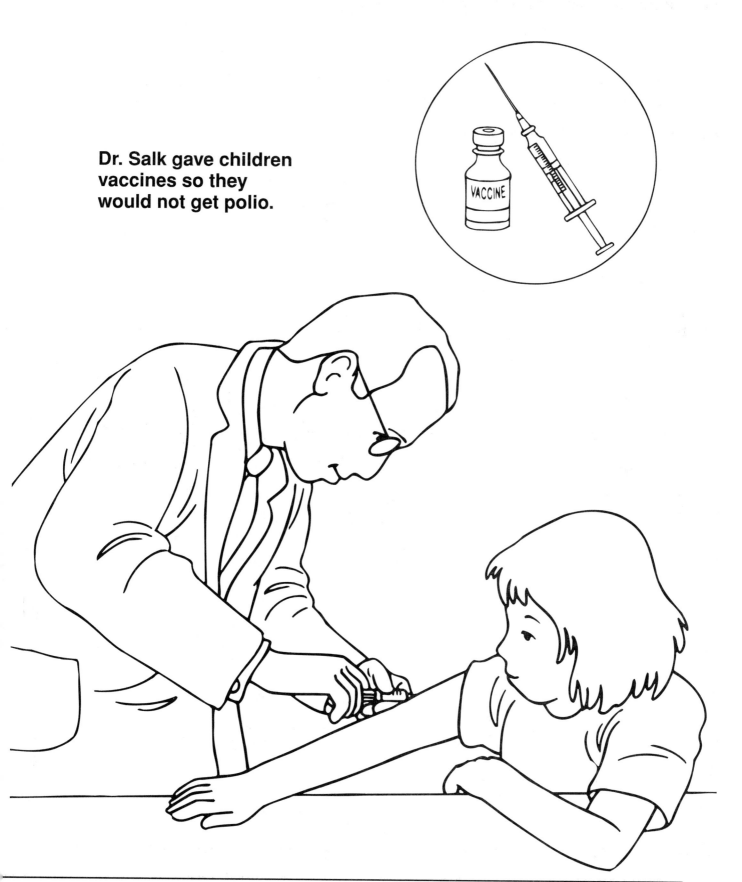

Dr. Salk gave children
vaccines so they
would not get polio.

Thank You, Dr. Salk

Kids were sick.
Some could not walk.

Dr. Salk helped.
He made a vaccine.

Lots of kids took the vaccine.
They did not get sick.

Thank you, Dr. Salk.

Nonfiction Reading Practice, Grade 1 • EMC 3312 • ©2003 by Evan-Moor Corp.

Name _____

Thank You, Dr. Salk

Fill in the bubble to complete each sentence.

1. Kids take a vaccine so they will <u>not</u> _____.
   - Ⓐ feel hot
   - Ⓑ get hungry
   - Ⓒ get sick

2. Some kids take a vaccine at _____.
   - Ⓐ the doctor's office
   - Ⓑ a party
   - Ⓒ the store

3. Dr. Salk made a vaccine to _____.
   - Ⓐ keep kids well
   - Ⓑ help kids walk
   - Ⓒ fix broken legs

Bonus: Draw or write about a time the doctor helped you.

A Good Doctor

Dr. Salk worked in his lab to make a polio vaccine.

Once there was a doctor. His name was Jonas Salk.
He saw kids with polio. Polio made kids sick.

Dr. Salk wanted to help. He went to his lab. He read.
He worked. He did not give up. He made a vaccine.

Kids took the vaccine. They did not get polio. Kids still
take the vaccine today. Jonas Salk was a good doctor.

Nonfiction Reading Practice, Grade 1 • EMC 3312 • ©2003 by Evan-Moor Corp.

Name _____

A Good Doctor

Fill in the bubble to answer each question or complete each sentence.

1. Dr. Jonas Salk worked in _____.
   - Ⓐ a class
   - Ⓑ a lab
   - Ⓒ a library

2. In the story, Dr. Jonas Salk did <u>not</u> _____.
   - Ⓐ make a vaccine
   - Ⓑ give up
   - Ⓒ get sick

3. Why did kids take the vaccine?
   - Ⓐ They didn't want to get a cold.
   - Ⓑ They didn't want to go to the doctor.
   - Ⓒ They didn't want to get polio.

Bonus: Write about why people remember Dr. Jonas Salk.

_____

_____

_____

_____

The Hero

Dr. Salk got a medal for making the polio vaccine.

Long ago, many people got polio. Some were a little bit sick. Some were very sick. Some could not walk. Some could not breathe. Some even died.

Dr. Jonas Salk wanted to help. He tried one thing. He tried another. He kept trying. Then he made something new. It was called a polio vaccine.

People took the vaccine. They did not get polio. The vaccine worked!

Now, people still take the vaccine. They do not want to get polio. Dr. Salk was a hero! He saved many lives.

Name _____

The Hero

Fill in the bubble to complete each sentence.

1. Dr. Jonas Salk made a vaccine _____.
   - Ⓐ the first time he tried
   - Ⓑ after many tries
   - Ⓒ only one time

2. A **hero** is someone we _____.
   - Ⓐ are proud of
   - Ⓑ don't know about
   - Ⓒ don't like

3. Dr. Salk got a medal because he _____.
   - Ⓐ saved children from getting polio
   - Ⓑ wanted people to be free
   - Ⓒ didn't get polio

Bonus: Write about someone else who is a hero to you.

_____

_____

_____

_____

Washing Hands

Introducing the Topic

1. Reproduce page 103 for individual students, or make a transparency to use with a group or your whole class.

2. Present the flow chart and discuss how people can prevent colds.

Reading the Selections

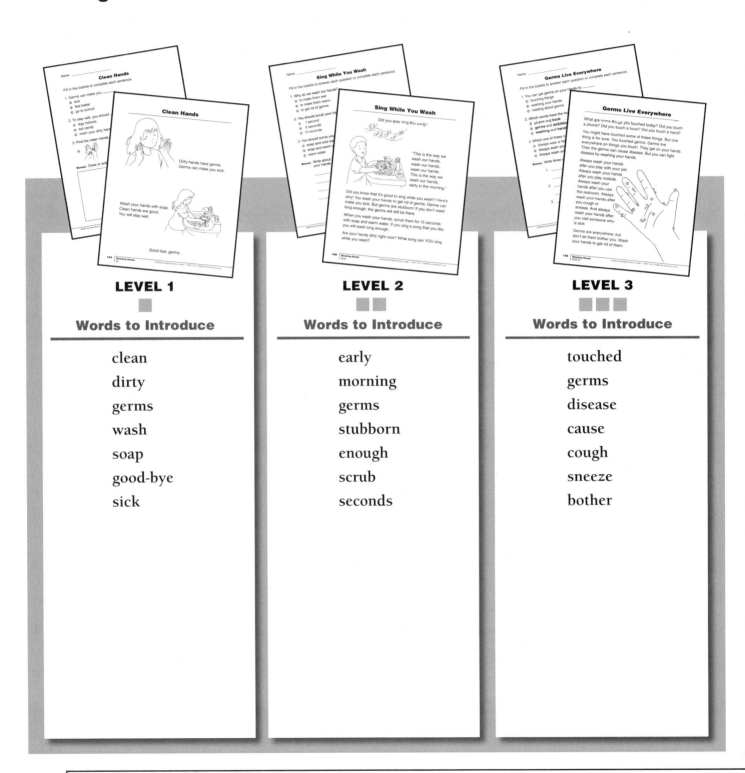

LEVEL 1	LEVEL 2	LEVEL 3
Words to Introduce	**Words to Introduce**	**Words to Introduce**
clean	early	touched
dirty	morning	germs
germs	germs	disease
wash	stubborn	cause
soap	enough	cough
good-bye	scrub	sneeze
sick	seconds	bother

Nonfiction Reading Practice, Grade 1 • EMC 3312 • ©2003 by Evan-Moor Corp.

Don't Get a Cold! Wash Your Hands!

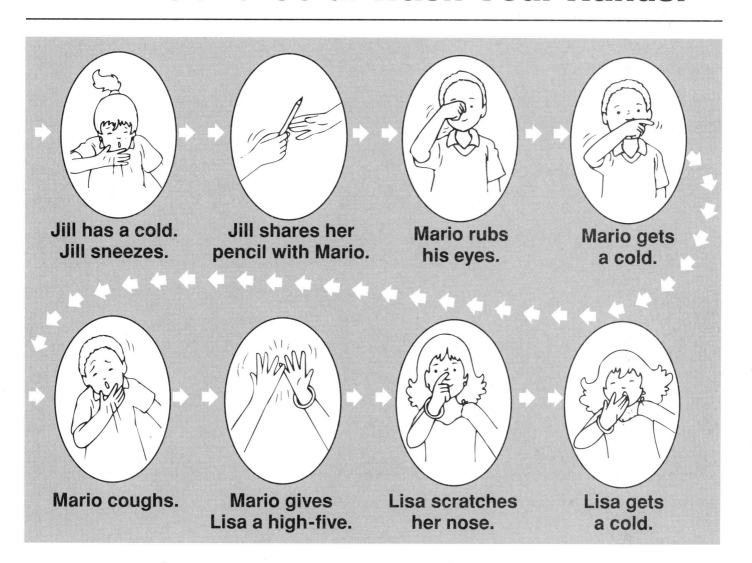

Jill has a cold.
Jill sneezes.

Jill shares her
pencil with Mario.

Mario rubs
his eyes.

Mario gets
a cold.

Mario coughs.

Mario gives
Lisa a high-five.

Lisa scratches
her nose.

Lisa gets
a cold.

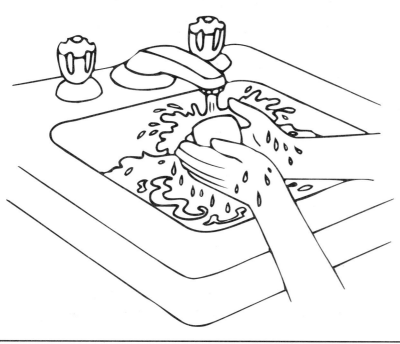

Friends can help each
other stay healthy. They
can wash their hands
with soap.

Clean Hands

Dirty hands have germs.
Germs can make you sick.

Wash your hands with soap.
Clean hands are good.
You will stay well.

Good-bye, germs.

Nonfiction Reading Practice, Grade 1 • EMC 3312 • ©2003 by Evan-Moor Corp.

Name _____

Clean Hands

Fill in the bubble to answer each question or complete each sentence.

1. Germs can make you _____.
   - Ⓐ sick
   - Ⓑ feel better
   - Ⓒ go to school

2. To stay well, you should _____.
   - Ⓐ stay indoors
   - Ⓑ eat candy
   - Ⓒ wash your dirty hands

3. Find the clean hands.

Ⓐ 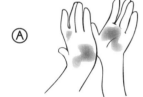   Ⓑ 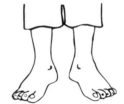   Ⓒ

Bonus: Draw or write about how your hands get dirty.

Sing While You Wash

Did you ever sing this song?

"This is the way we wash our hands, wash our hands, wash our hands. This is the way we wash our hands, early in the morning."

Did you know that it's good to sing while you wash? Here's why! You wash your hands to get rid of germs. Germs can make you sick. But germs are stubborn! If you don't wash long enough, the germs will still be there.

When you wash your hands, scrub them for 15 seconds with soap and warm water. If you sing a song that you like, you will wash long enough.

Are your hands dirty right now? What song can YOU sing while you wash?

   Nonfiction Reading Practice, Grade 1 • EMC 3312 • ©2003 by Evan-Moor Corp.

Name _____

Sing While You Wash

Fill in the bubble to answer each question or complete each sentence.

1. Why do we wash our hands?
   - Ⓐ to make them wet
   - Ⓑ to make them warm
   - Ⓒ to get rid of germs

2. You should scrub your hands for at least _____.
   - Ⓐ 1 second
   - Ⓑ 5 seconds
   - Ⓒ 15 seconds

3. You should scrub your hands with _____.
   - Ⓐ soap and cold water
   - Ⓑ soap and warm water
   - Ⓒ warm water

Bonus: Write about another good song to sing while you wash your hands.

_____

_____

_____

_____

Germs Live Everywhere

What are some things you touched today? Did you touch a phone? Did you touch a book? Did you touch a hand?

You might have touched some of these things. But one thing is for sure. You touched germs. Germs live everywhere on things you touch. They get on your hands. Then the germs can cause disease. But you can fight disease by washing your hands.

Always wash your hands after you play with your pet. Always wash your hands after you play outside. Always wash your hands after you use the restroom. Always wash your hands after you cough or sneeze. And always wash your hands after you visit someone who is sick.

Germs are everywhere, but don't let them bother you. Wash your hands to get rid of them.

Nonfiction Reading Practice, Grade 1 • EMC 3312 • ©2003 by Evan-Moor Corp.

Name _____

Germs Live Everywhere

Fill in the bubble to answer each question or complete each sentence.

1. You can get germs on your hands by _____.
   - Ⓐ touching things
   - Ⓑ washing your hands
   - Ⓒ reading about germs

2. Which words have the most to do with disease?
   - Ⓐ **phone** and **book**
   - Ⓑ **germs** and **sickness**
   - Ⓒ **washing** and **hands**

3. Which one of these rules will help you <u>not</u> get a disease?
   - Ⓐ Always wear a helmet when you ride your bike.
   - Ⓑ Always wash your clothes before you wear them.
   - Ⓒ Always wash your hands after you cough or sneeze.

Bonus: Write three rules to follow about washing your hands.

1. _____

   _____

2. _____

   _____

3. _____

   _____

Money

Introducing the Topic

1. Reproduce page 111 for individual students, or make a transparency to use with a group or your whole class.

2. Present the picture of the boy with his piggy bank. Discuss that money can be both coins and bills.

Reading the Selections

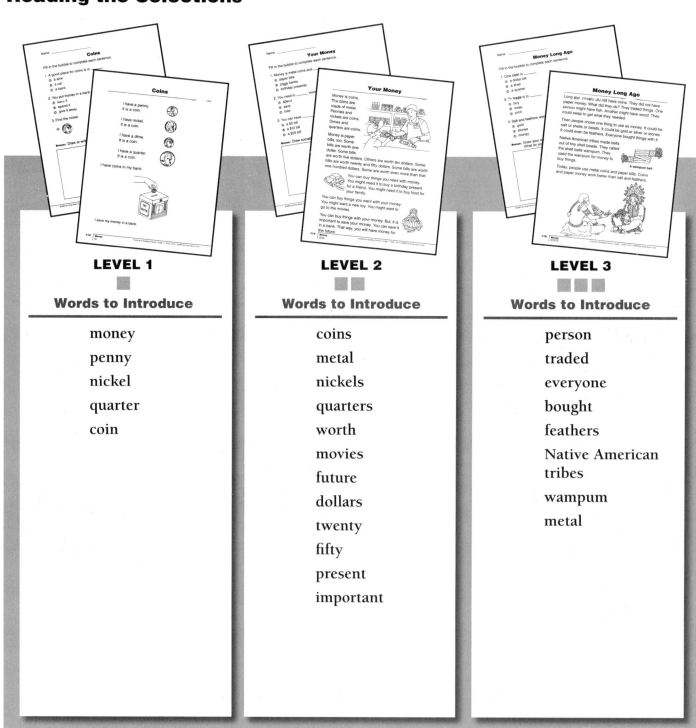

LEVEL 1

Words to Introduce

money

penny

nickel

quarter

coin

LEVEL 2

Words to Introduce

coins

metal

nickels

quarters

worth

movies

future

dollars

twenty

fifty

present

important

LEVEL 3

Words to Introduce

person

traded

everyone

bought

feathers

Native American tribes

wampum

metal

Nonfiction Reading Practice, Grade 1 • EMC 3312 • ©2003 by Evan-Moor Corp.

Money

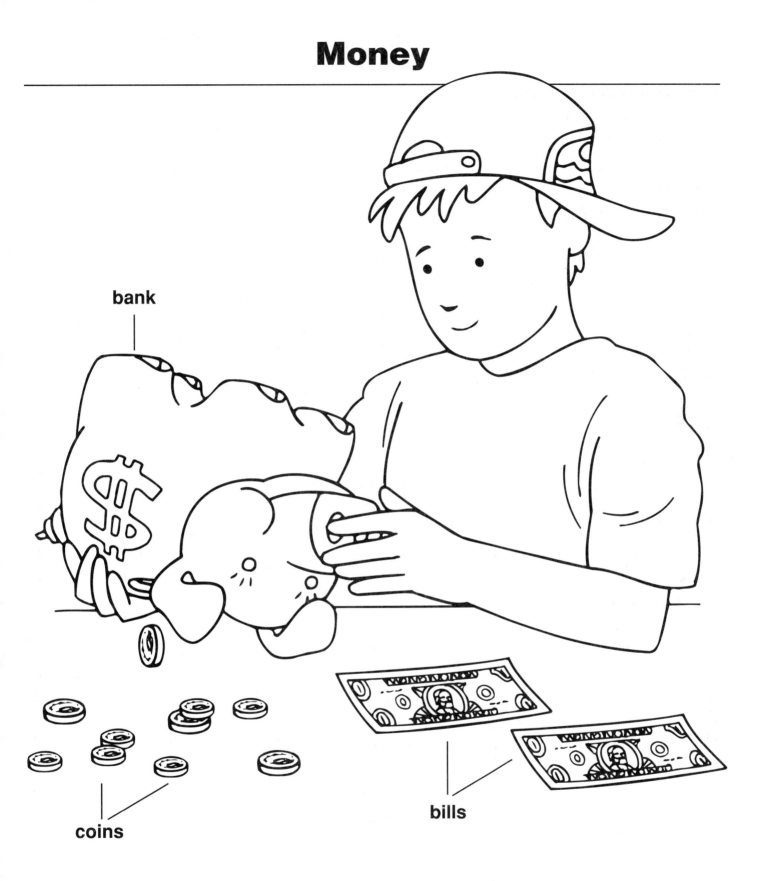

bank

coins

bills

This boy keeps his money in a piggy bank.

Coins

I have a penny.
It is a coin.

I have nickel.
It is a coin.

I have a dime.
It is a coin.

I have a quarter.
It is a coin.

I have coins in my bank.

I save my money in a bank.

Nonfiction Reading Practice, Grade 1 • EMC 3312 • ©2003 by Evan-Moor Corp.

Name _____

Coins

Fill in the bubble to answer each question or complete each sentence.

1. A good place for coins is in _____.
   - Ⓐ a sink
   - Ⓑ a car
   - Ⓒ a bank

2. You put money in a bank to _____.
   - Ⓐ save it
   - Ⓑ spend it
   - Ⓒ give it away

3. Find the nickel.

Ⓐ    Ⓑ   Ⓒ

Bonus: Draw or write about where you save your coins.

Your Money

Money is coins. The coins are made of metal. Pennies and nickels are coins. Dimes and quarters are coins.

Money is paper bills, too. Some bills are worth one dollar. Some bills are worth five dollars. Others are worth ten dollars. Some bills are worth twenty and fifty dollars. Some are worth even more than that.

You can buy things you need with money. You might need it to buy a birthday present for a friend. You might need it to buy food for your family.

You can buy things you want with your money. You might want a new toy. You might want to go to the movies.

You can buy things with your money. But, it is important to save your money. You can save it in a bank. That way, you will have money for the future.

Nonfiction Reading Practice, Grade 1 • EMC 3312 • ©2003 by Evan-Moor Corp.

Name _____

Your Money

Fill in the bubble to complete each sentence.

1. **Money** is metal coins and _____.
   - Ⓐ paper bills
   - Ⓑ piggy banks
   - Ⓒ birthday presents

2. You need to _____ money for the future.
   - Ⓐ spend
   - Ⓑ save
   - Ⓒ lose

3. You can have _____.
   - Ⓐ a $5 bill
   - Ⓑ a $12 bill
   - Ⓒ a $25 bill

Bonus: Draw something you want to buy. How much does it cost?

Money Long Ago

Long ago, people did not have coins. They did not have paper money. What did they do? They traded things. One person might have fish. Another might have wood. They could swap to get what they needed.

Then people chose one thing to use as money. It could be salt or shells or beads. It could be gold or silver or stones. It could even be feathers. Everyone bought things with it.

Native American tribes made belts out of tiny shell beads. They called the shell belts wampum. They used the wampum as money to buy things.

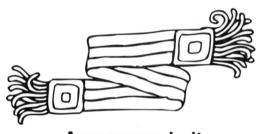

A wampum belt

Today, people use metal coins and paper bills. Coins and paper money work better than fish and feathers.

Nonfiction Reading Practice, Grade 1 • EMC 3312 • ©2003 by Evan-Moor Corp.

Name _____

Money Long Ago

Fill in the bubble to complete each sentence.

1. One **coin** is _____.
   - Ⓐ a dollar bill
   - Ⓑ a shell
   - Ⓒ a quarter

2. To **trade** is to _____.
   - Ⓐ buy
   - Ⓑ swap
   - Ⓒ print

3. Fish and feathers were once used as _____.
   - Ⓐ gold
   - Ⓑ stones
   - Ⓒ money

Bonus: Draw your own kind of wampum belt to use as money. What do you call your money?

Time

Introducing the Topic

1. Reproduce page 119 for individual students, or make a transparency to use with a group or your whole class.

2. Present the clock pictures. Read and discuss the different kinds of clocks.

Reading the Selections

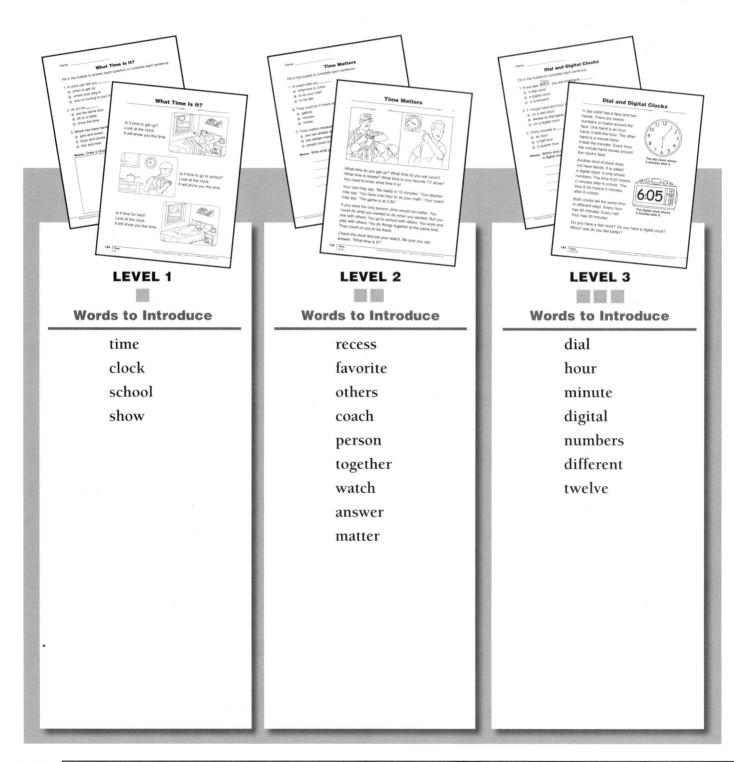

LEVEL 1	LEVEL 2	LEVEL 3
■	■ ■	■ ■ ■
Words to Introduce	**Words to Introduce**	**Words to Introduce**
time	recess	dial
clock	favorite	hour
school	others	minute
show	coach	digital
	person	numbers
	together	different
	watch	twelve
	answer	
	matter	

Time

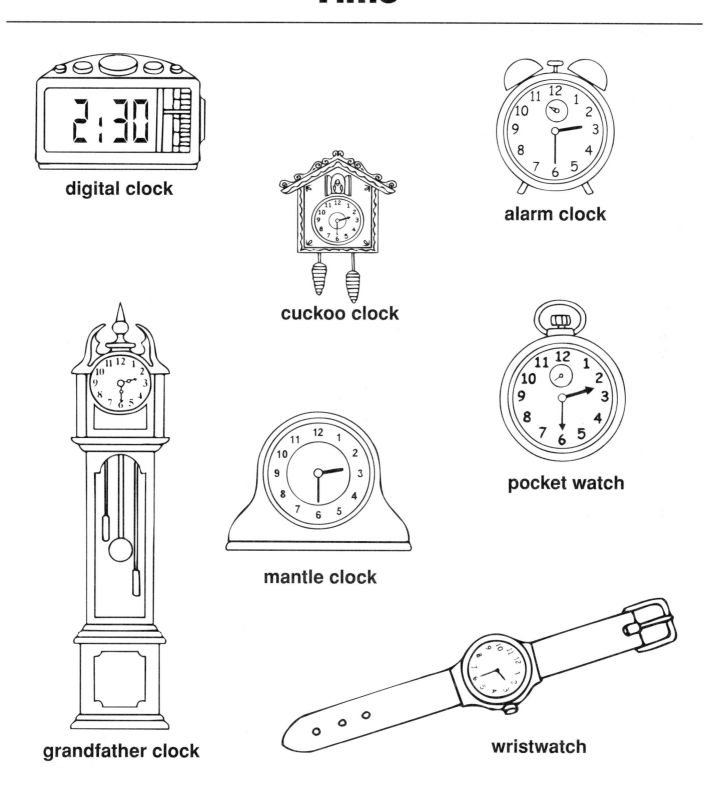

digital clock

cuckoo clock

alarm clock

grandfather clock

mantle clock

pocket watch

wristwatch

There are many different kinds of clocks.

What Time Is It?

Is it time to get up?
Look at the clock.
It will show you the time.

Is it time to go to school?
Look at the clock.
It will show you the time.

Is it time for bed?
Look at the clock.
It will show you the time.

Nonfiction Reading Practice, Grade 1 • EMC 3312 • ©2003 by Evan-Moor Corp.

Name _____

What Time Is It?

Fill in the bubble to answer each question or complete each sentence.

1. A clock can tell you _____.
   - Ⓐ when to get up
   - Ⓑ where your dog is
   - Ⓒ who is coming to your house

2. All clocks _____.
   - Ⓐ are the same size
   - Ⓑ sit on a table
   - Ⓒ show the time

3. Which two have hands?
   - Ⓐ girls and books
   - Ⓑ boys and clocks
   - Ⓒ fish and men

Bonus: Draw a clock you have at home.

Time Matters

What time do you get up? What time do you eat lunch? What time is recess? What time is your favorite TV show? You need to know what time it is!

Your dad may say, "Be ready in 10 minutes." Your teacher may say, "You have one hour to do your math." Your coach may say, "The game is at 5:30."

If you were the only person, time would not matter. You could do what you wanted to do when you wanted. But you live with others. You go to school with others. You work and play with others. You do things together at the same time. They count on you to be there.

Check the clock and set your watch. Be sure you can answer, "What time is it?"

Nonfiction Reading Practice, Grade 1 • EMC 3312 • ©2003 by Evan-Moor Corp.

Name _____

Time Matters

Fill in the bubble to complete each sentence.

1. A coach tells you _____.
   Ⓐ what time to come
   Ⓑ to do your math
   Ⓒ to be late

2. Time is in hours and _____.
   Ⓐ gallons
   Ⓑ minutes
   Ⓒ inches

3. Time matters because _____.
   Ⓐ you can always do what you want
   Ⓑ you always need to hurry
   Ⓒ people count on you to be on time

Bonus: Write what you like to do at 4:00 in the afternoon.

_____

_____

_____

_____

Dial and Digital Clocks

A dial clock has a face and two hands. There are twelve numbers or marks around the face. One hand is an hour hand. It tells the hour. The other hand is a minute hand. It tells the minutes. Every hour, the minute hand moves around the clock's face.

The dial clock shows 5 minutes after 6.

Another kind of clock does not have hands. It is called a digital clock. It only shows numbers. The time 6:02 means 2 minutes after 6 o'clock. The time 6:05 means 5 minutes after 6 o'clock.

The digital clock shows 5 minutes after 6.

Both clocks tell the same time in different ways. Every hour has 60 minutes. Every half hour has 30 minutes.

Do you have a dial clock? Do you have a digital clock? Which one do you like better?

Nonfiction Reading Practice, Grade 1 • EMC 3312 • ©2003 by Evan-Moor Corp.

Name _____

Dial and Digital Clocks

Fill in the bubble to complete each sentence.

1. If you see [6:05], you are looking at _____.

   Ⓐ a dial clock

   Ⓑ a digital clock

   Ⓒ a wristwatch

2. A minute hand and an hour hand are _____.

   Ⓐ on a dial clock

   Ⓑ always on the same number

   Ⓒ on a digital clock

3. Thirty minutes is _____.

   Ⓐ an hour

   Ⓑ a half hour

   Ⓒ a quarter hour

Bonus: Which kind of clock do you like better—a dial clock or a digital clock? Why?

_____

_____

_____

_____

Calendars

Introducing the Topic

1. Reproduce page 127 for individual students, or make a transparency to use with a group or your whole class.

2. Present the labeled calendar. Read and discuss the calendar, labels, and caption.

Reading the Selections

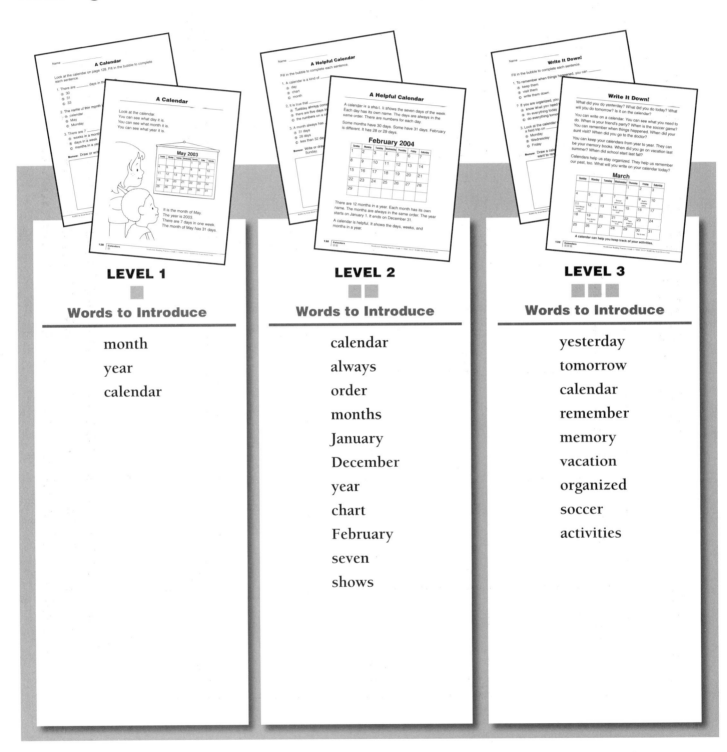

LEVEL 1

Words to Introduce

month

year

calendar

LEVEL 2

Words to Introduce

calendar

always

order

months

January

December

year

chart

February

seven

shows

LEVEL 3

Words to Introduce

yesterday

tomorrow

calendar

remember

memory

vacation

organized

soccer

activities

Nonfiction Reading Practice, Grade 1 • EMC 3312 • ©2003 by Evan-Moor Corp.

November —— Month

Day of Week

Sunday	Monday	Tuesday	Wednesday	Thursday	Friday	Saturday
					1	2
3	4	5	6	7	8	9
10	11	12	13	14	15	16
17	18	19	20	21	22	23
24	25	26	27	28	29	30

A calendar tells us which day of the week it is and which day of the month it is. Look at this calendar. On what day of the week is November 12? What days of the month fall on Saturdays?

A Calendar

Look at the calendar.
You can see what day it is.
You can see what month it is.
You can see what year it is.

May 2003

Sunday	Monday	Tuesday	Wednesday	Thursday	Friday	Saturday
				1	2	3
4	5	6	7	8	9	10
11	12	13	14	15	16	17
18	19	20	21	22	23	24
25	26	27	28	29	30	31

It is the month of May.
The year is 2003.
There are 7 days in one week.
The month of May has 31 days.

Name _____

A Calendar

Look at the calendar on page 128. Fill in the bubble to complete each sentence.

1. There are _____ days in this month.
   - Ⓐ 30
   - Ⓑ 31
   - Ⓒ 33

2. The name of this month is _____.
   - Ⓐ calendar
   - Ⓑ May
   - Ⓒ Monday

3. There are 7 _____.
   - Ⓐ weeks in a month
   - Ⓑ days in a week
   - Ⓒ months in a year

Bonus: Draw or write about the day of the week you like best.

A Helpful Calendar

A calendar is a chart. It shows the seven days of the week. Each day has its own name. The days are always in the same order. There are numbers for each day.

Some months have 30 days. Some have 31 days. February is different. It has 28 or 29 days.

February 2004

Sunday	Monday	Tuesday	Wednesday	Thursday	Friday	Saturday
1	2	3	4	5	6	7
8	9	10	11	12	13	14
15	16	17	18	19	20	21
22	23	24	25	26	27	28
29						

There are 12 months in a year. Each month has its own name. The months are always in the same order. The year starts on January 1. It ends on December 31.

A calendar is helpful. It shows the days, weeks, and months in a year.

Nonfiction Reading Practice, Grade 1 • EMC 3312 • ©2003 by Evan-Moor Corp.

Name _____

A Helpful Calendar

Fill in the bubble to complete each sentence.

1. A **calendar** is a kind of _____.
   - Ⓐ day
   - Ⓑ chart
   - Ⓒ month

2. It is true that _____.
   - Ⓐ Tuesday always comes after Monday
   - Ⓑ there are five days in a week
   - Ⓒ the numbers on a calendar stand for months

3. A month always has _____.
   - Ⓐ 31 days
   - Ⓑ 28 days
   - Ⓒ less than 32 days

Bonus: Write or draw one thing you might do on Saturday and Sunday.

Write It Down!

What did you do yesterday? What did you do today? What will you do tomorrow? Is it on the calendar?

You can write on a calendar. You can see what you need to do. When is your friend's party? When is the soccer game? You can remember when things happened. When did your aunt visit? When did you go to the doctor?

You can keep your calendars from year to year. They can be your memory books. When did you go on vacation last summer? When did school start last fall?

Calendars help us stay organized. They help us remember our past, too. What will you write on your calendar today?

March

Sunday	Monday	Tuesday	Wednesday	Thursday	Friday	Saturday
			1	2	3	
4	5	6	7 Soccer game 5:00	8	9 Sudi's birthday party	10
11 Aunt Marge coming to visit	12	13	14 Soccer game 5:00	15	16	17
18	19 Eye doctor 3:00	20	21 Soccer game 5:00	22 Take treats to school	23	24
25	26	27	28	29	30 Trip to zoo	31

A calendar can help you keep track of your activities.

Nonfiction Reading Practice, Grade 1 • EMC 3312 • ©2003 by Evan-Moor Corp.

Name _____

Write It Down!

Fill in the bubble to complete each sentence.

1. To remember when things happened, you can _____.
   - Ⓐ keep them
   - Ⓑ visit them
   - Ⓒ write them down

2. If you are **organized**, you _____.
   - Ⓐ know what you need to do
   - Ⓑ do everything today
   - Ⓒ do everything tomorrow

3. Look at the calendar on page 132. The children are going on a field trip on _____.
   - Ⓐ Monday
   - Ⓑ Wednesday
   - Ⓒ Friday

Bonus: Draw a calendar for this week. Write in one thing you want to remember.

Cave Art

Introducing the Topic

1. Reproduce page 135 for individual students, or make a transparency to use with a group or your whole class.

2. Present the cave art animal sketches. Read and discuss the caption.

Reading the Selections

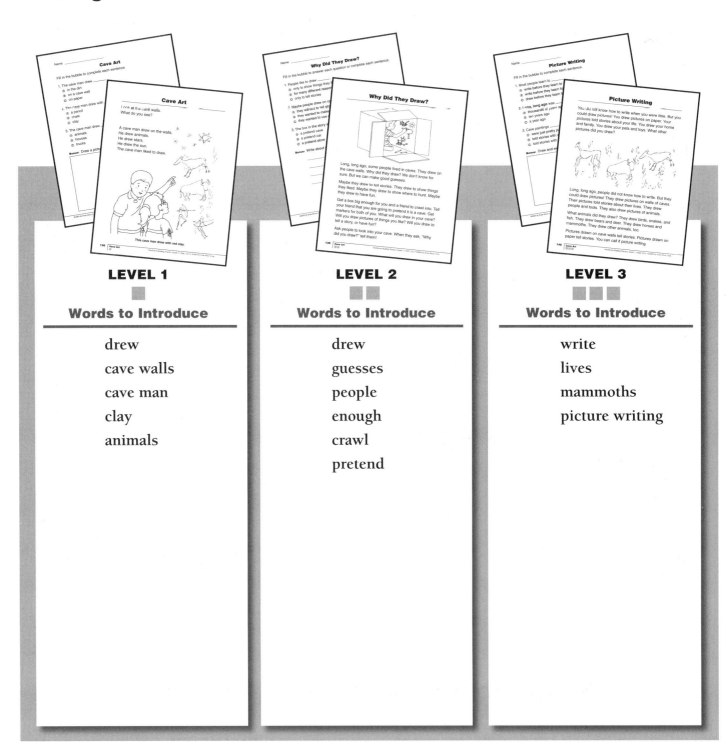

LEVEL 1
■

Words to Introduce

drew

cave walls

cave man

clay

animals

LEVEL 2
■ ■

Words to Introduce

drew

guesses

people

enough

crawl

pretend

LEVEL 3
■ ■ ■

Words to Introduce

write

lives

mammoths

picture writing

Nonfiction Reading Practice, Grade 1 • EMC 3312 • ©2003 by Evan-Moor Corp.

Cave Art

Long ago, people drew pictures on the walls of caves.

Cave Art

Look at the cave walls.
What do you see?

A cave man drew on the walls.
He drew animals.
He drew stars.
He drew the sun.
The cave man liked to draw.

This cave man drew with red clay.

Nonfiction Reading Practice, Grade 1 • EMC 3312 • ©2003 by Evan-Moor Corp.

Name _____

Cave Art

Fill in the bubble to complete each sentence.

1. The cave man drew _____.
   - Ⓐ in the dirt
   - Ⓑ on a cave wall
   - Ⓒ on paper

2. The cave man drew with _____.
   - Ⓐ a pencil
   - Ⓑ chalk
   - Ⓒ clay

3. The cave man drew _____.
   - Ⓐ animals
   - Ⓑ houses
   - Ⓒ trucks

Bonus: Draw a picture of you and your pet on a pretend cave wall.

Why Did They Draw?

Long, long ago, some people lived in caves. They drew on the cave walls. Why did they draw? We don't know for sure. But we can make good guesses.

Maybe they drew to tell stories. They drew to show things they liked. Maybe they drew to show where to hunt. Maybe they drew to have fun.

Get a box big enough for you and a friend to crawl into. Tell your friend that you are going to pretend it is a cave. Get markers for both of you. What will you draw in your cave? Will you draw pictures of things you like? Will you draw to tell a story, or have fun?

Ask people to look into your cave. When they ask, "Why did you draw?" tell them!

Why Did They Draw?

Fill in the bubble to answer each question or complete each sentence.

1. People like to draw _____.
   - Ⓐ only to show things they like
   - Ⓑ for many different reasons
   - Ⓒ only to tell stories

2. Maybe people drew on cave walls because they wanted _____.
   - Ⓐ to tell stories with pictures
   - Ⓑ to make good guesses
   - Ⓒ to use markers

3. The box in the story was a pretend _____.
   - Ⓐ cave
   - Ⓑ car
   - Ⓒ store

Bonus: Write about what you would draw on a cave wall.

_____

_____

_____

_____

Picture Writing

You did not know how to write when you were little. But you could draw pictures! You drew pictures on paper. Your pictures told stories about your life. You drew your home and family. You drew your pets and toys. What other pictures did you draw?

Long, long ago, people did not know how to write. But they could draw pictures! They drew pictures on walls of caves. Their pictures told stories about their lives. They drew people and tools. They also drew pictures of animals.

What animals did they draw? They drew birds, snakes, and fish. They drew bears and deer. They drew horses and mammoths. They drew other animals, too.

Pictures drawn on cave walls tell stories. Pictures drawn on paper tell stories. You can call it picture writing.

Nonfiction Reading Practice, Grade 1 • EMC 3312 • ©2003 by Evan-Moor Corp.

Name _____

Picture Writing

Fill in the bubble to complete each sentence.

1. Most people learn to _____.
   - Ⓐ write before they learn to draw
   - Ⓑ write before they learn to tell stories
   - Ⓒ draw before they learn to write

2. **Long, long ago** was _____.
   - Ⓐ thousands of years ago
   - Ⓑ ten years ago
   - Ⓒ a year ago

3. Cave paintings _____.
   - Ⓐ were just pretty pictures
   - Ⓑ told stories with words
   - Ⓒ told stories with pictures

Bonus: Draw and write a story about what is special to you.

Folk Music

Introducing the Topic

1. Reproduce page 143 for individual students, or make a transparency to use with a group or your whole class.

2. Present the "Ring Around the Rosy" folk song game sheet. Read and discuss the caption.

Reading the Selections

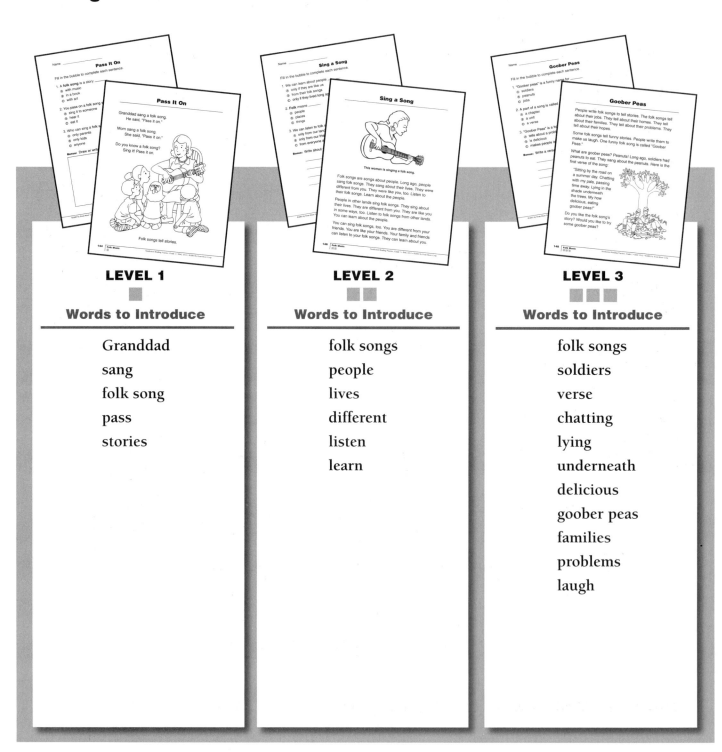

LEVEL 1

Words to Introduce

Granddad

sang

folk song

pass

stories

LEVEL 2

Words to Introduce

folk songs

people

lives

different

listen

learn

LEVEL 3

Words to Introduce

folk songs

soldiers

verse

chatting

lying

underneath

delicious

goober peas

families

problems

laugh

Folk Music

Ring around the Rosy,

Pocket full of posies,

Ashes, ashes,

We all fall down.

Have you ever played the folk song game "Ring Around the Rosy"?

Pass It On

Granddad sang a folk song.
    He said, "Pass it on."

Mom sang a folk song.
    She said, "Pass it on."

Do you know a folk song?
    Sing it! Pass it on.

Folk songs tell stories.

Nonfiction Reading Practice, Grade 1 • EMC 3312 • ©2003 by Evan-Moor Corp.

Name _____

Pass It On

Fill in the bubble to answer each question or complete each sentence.

1. A **folk song** is a story _____.
   - Ⓐ with music
   - Ⓑ in a book
   - Ⓒ with art

2. You **pass on** a folk song when you _____.
   - Ⓐ sing it to someone
   - Ⓑ hear it
   - Ⓒ eat it

3. Who can sing a folk song?
   - Ⓐ only parents
   - Ⓑ only kids
   - Ⓒ anyone

Bonus: Draw or write about a song you like.

Sing a Song

This woman is singing a folk song.

Folk songs are songs about people. Long ago, people sang folk songs. They sang about their lives. They were different from you. They were like you, too. Listen to their folk songs. Learn about the people.

People in other lands sing folk songs. They sing about their lives. They are different from you. They are like you in some ways, too. Listen to folk songs from other lands. You can learn about the people.

You can sing folk songs, too. You are different from your friends. You are like your friends. Your family and friends can listen to your folk songs. They can learn about you.

Nonfiction Reading Practice, Grade 1 • EMC 3312 • ©2003 by Evan-Moor Corp.

Name _____

Sing a Song

Fill in the bubble to complete each sentence.

1. We can learn about people _____.
   - Ⓐ only if they are like us
   - Ⓑ from their folk songs
   - Ⓒ only if they lived long ago

2. **Folk** means _____.
   - Ⓐ people
   - Ⓑ places
   - Ⓒ things

3. We can listen to folk songs _____.
   - Ⓐ only from our land
   - Ⓑ only from our friends
   - Ⓒ from everyone and everywhere

Bonus: Write about someone you know who sings folk songs.

_____

_____

_____

_____

Goober Peas

People write folk songs to tell stories. The folk songs tell about their jobs. They tell about their homes. They tell about their families. They tell about their problems. They tell about their hopes.

Some folk songs tell funny stories. People write them to make us laugh. One funny folk song is called "Goober Peas."

What are goober peas? Peanuts! Long ago, soldiers had peanuts to eat. They sang about the peanuts. Here is the first verse of the song:

"Sitting by the road on a summer day. Chatting with my pals, passing time away. Lying in the shade underneath the trees. My how delicious, eating goober peas!"

Do you like the folk song's story? Would you like to try some goober peas?

Nonfiction Reading Practice, Grade 1 • EMC 3312 • ©2003 by Evan-Moor Corp.

Name _____

Goober Peas

Fill in the bubble to complete each sentence.

1. "Goober peas" is a funny name for _____.
   - Ⓐ soldiers
   - Ⓑ peanuts
   - Ⓒ jobs

2. A **part of a song** is called _____.
   - Ⓐ a chapter
   - Ⓑ a unit
   - Ⓒ a verse

3. "Goober Peas" is a folk song that _____.
   - Ⓐ tells about a problem
   - Ⓑ is delicious
   - Ⓒ makes people laugh

Bonus: Write a verse for a funny song about a food you like.

_____

_____

_____

_____

Houses

Introducing the Topic

1. Reproduce page 151 for individual students, or make a transparency to use with a group or your whole class.

2. Present the drawings of different kinds of houses. Read and discuss the captions.

Reading the Selections

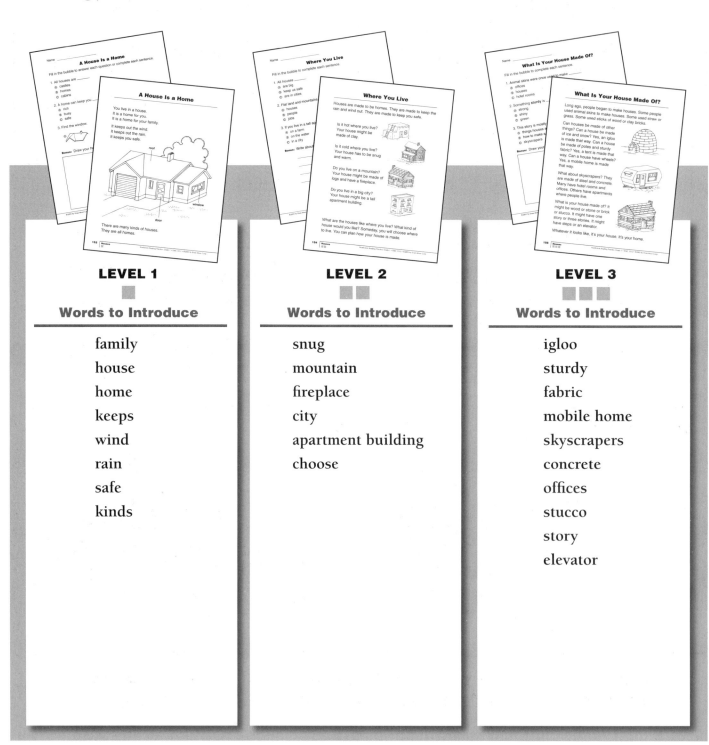

LEVEL 1	**LEVEL 2**	**LEVEL 3**
Words to Introduce	**Words to Introduce**	**Words to Introduce**
family	snug	igloo
house	mountain	sturdy
home	fireplace	fabric
keeps	city	mobile home
wind	apartment building	skyscrapers
rain	choose	concrete
safe		offices
kinds		stucco
		story
		elevator

Nonfiction Reading Practice, Grade 1 • EMC 3312 • ©2003 by Evan-Moor Corp.

Different Kinds of Houses

log cabin

adobe house

apartment

mobile home

brick house

houseboat

Here are six different kinds of houses. In what ways are they like your home? In what ways are they different from your home?

A House Is a Home

You live in a house.
It is a home for you.
It is a home for your family.

It keeps out the wind.
It keeps out the rain.
It keeps you safe.

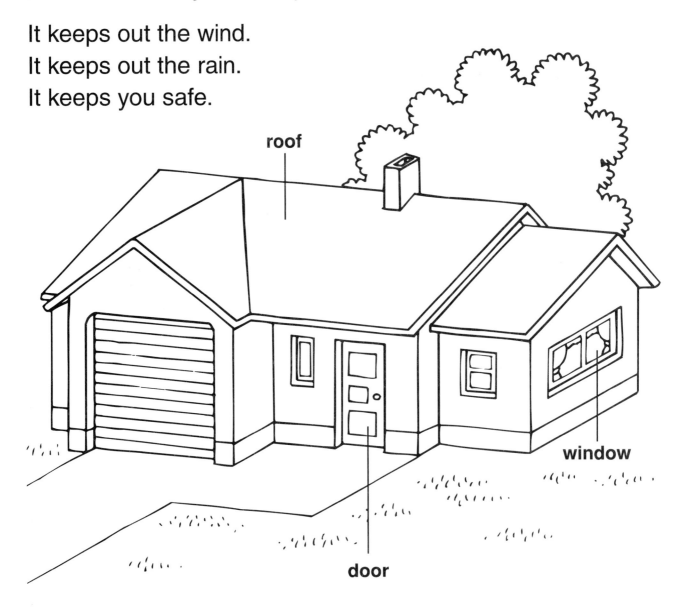

roof

window

door

There are many kinds of houses.
They are all homes.

Nonfiction Reading Practice, Grade 1 • EMC 3312 • ©2003 by Evan-Moor Corp.

Name _____

A House Is a Home

Fill in the bubble to answer each question or complete each sentence.

1. All houses are _____.
   - Ⓐ castles
   - Ⓑ homes
   - Ⓒ cabins

2. A home can keep you _____.
   - Ⓐ rich
   - Ⓑ busy
   - Ⓒ safe

3. Find the window.

Ⓐ 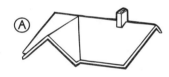   Ⓑ   Ⓒ

Bonus: Draw your house.

Where You Live

Houses are made to be homes. They are made to keep the rain and wind out. They are made to keep you safe.

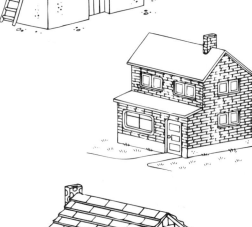

Is it hot where you live?
Your house might be
made of clay.

Is it cold where you live?
Your house has to be snug
and warm.

Do you live on a mountain?
Your house might be made of
logs and have a fireplace.

Do you live in a big city?
Your house might be a tall
apartment building.

What are the houses like where you live? What kind of house would you like? Someday, you will choose where to live. You can plan how your house is made.

Nonfiction Reading Practice, Grade 1 • EMC 3312 • ©2003 by Evan-Moor Corp.

Name _____

Where You Live

Fill in the bubble to complete each sentence.

1. All houses _____.
   - Ⓐ are big
   - Ⓑ keep us safe
   - Ⓒ are in cities

2. Flat land and mountains need different kinds of _____.
   - Ⓐ houses
   - Ⓑ people
   - Ⓒ jobs

3. If you live in a tall apartment building, you may live _____.
   - Ⓐ on a farm
   - Ⓑ on the water
   - Ⓒ in a city

Bonus: Write about a house that would be fun to live in.

_____

_____

_____

_____

What Is Your House Made Of?

Long ago, people began to make houses. Some people used animal skins to make houses. Some used straw or grass. Some used sticks of wood or clay bricks.

Can houses be made of other things? Can a house be made of ice and snow? Yes, an igloo is made that way. Can a house be made of poles and sturdy fabric? Yes, a tent is made that way. Can a house have wheels? Yes, a mobile home is made that way.

What about skyscrapers? They are made of steel and concrete. Many have hotel rooms and offices. Others have apartments where people live.

What is your house made of? It might be wood or stone or brick or stucco. It might have one story or three stories. It might have steps or an elevator.

Whatever it looks like, it's your house. It's your home.

Nonfiction Reading Practice, Grade 1 • EMC 3312 • ©2003 by Evan-Moor Corp.

Name _____

What Is Your House Made Of?

Fill in the bubble to complete each sentence.

1. Animal skins were once used to make _____.
   - Ⓐ offices
   - Ⓑ houses
   - Ⓒ hotel rooms

2. Something **sturdy** is _____.
   - Ⓐ strong
   - Ⓑ shiny
   - Ⓒ green

3. This story is mostly about _____.
   - Ⓐ things houses are made of
   - Ⓑ how to make a toy house
   - Ⓒ skyscrapers

Bonus: Draw your dream house. What is it made of?

Puppets

Introducing the Topic

1. Reproduce page 159 for individual students, or make a transparency to use with a group or your whole class.

2. Tell students that people from all over the world love puppets. Make a list of all the different kinds of puppets students have seen. Students will probably list finger, sock, and paper bag puppets.

Reading the Selections

LEVEL 1

Words to Introduce

puppet

now

talk

move

fingers

LEVEL 2

Words to Introduce

else

cloth

move

finger

table

stage

chair

know

LEVEL 3

Words to Introduce

marionettes

bodies

laugh

voice

Nonfiction Reading Practice, Grade 1 • EMC 3312 • ©2003 by Evan-Moor Corp.

Many Kinds of Puppets

Finger Puppet

Sock Puppet

Stick Puppet

Bag Puppet

Sock Puppet

It was a sock.
Now it is a puppet.

Put it on your hand.
Move your fingers.

You can make your
puppet talk.

What will the puppet say?

Nonfiction Reading Practice, Grade 1 • EMC 3312 • ©2003 by Evan-Moor Corp.

Name _____

Sock Puppet

Fill in the bubble to complete each sentence.

1. A sock puppet goes on your _____.
   - Ⓐ foot
   - Ⓑ head
   - Ⓒ hand

2. The boy made the sock puppet _____.
   - Ⓐ move
   - Ⓑ listen
   - Ⓒ grow

3. The boy's sock puppet has _____ for eyes.
   - Ⓐ dots
   - Ⓑ buttons
   - Ⓒ pins

Bonus: Draw or write about a puppet you like.

All About Puppets

A puppet can be a cat.
A puppet can be a king.
A puppet can be a tree.
What else can a puppet be?

A puppet can be made of paper.
A puppet can be made of cloth.
A puppet can be made of wood.
What else can a puppet be made of?

A stick can make a puppet move.
A string can make a puppet move.
A finger can make a puppet move.
What else can make a puppet move?

A table can be a puppet stage.
A box can be a puppet stage.
A chair can be a puppet stage.
What else can be a puppet stage?

What else do you know
about puppets?

Name _____

All About Puppets

Fill in the bubble to answer each question or complete each sentence.

1. Can a puppet be made of wood?

   Ⓐ yes

   Ⓑ no

   Ⓒ sometimes

2. A **stage** is a place to _____.

   Ⓐ make something

   Ⓑ put on a show

   Ⓒ keep things

3. What else do you know about puppets?

   Ⓐ Puppets are toys.

   Ⓑ Puppets are tools.

   Ⓒ Puppets are pets.

Bonus: Write about a puppet you have played with.

_____

_____

_____

_____

Little Mary

People have fun with puppets. Some kinds are hand puppets. Some kinds are rod puppets. Some kinds are marionettes. **Marionette** means "Little Mary."

Marionettes have heads and bodies. They have arms and legs. They have hands and feet. They have strings to make them move. People use them to tell stories. People use them to make people laugh.

Could you use one to tell a story? Could you use one to sing a song? Could you give Little Mary a funny voice?

Have fun with a hand puppet. Have fun with a rod puppet. But have the most fun with a Little Mary!

You make a marionette move by pulling the strings.

Nonfiction Reading Practice, Grade 1 • EMC 3312 • ©2003 by Evan-Moor Corp.

Name _____

Little Mary

Fill in the bubble to complete each sentence.

1. Puppets can be different _____.
   - Ⓐ kinds
   - Ⓑ rods
   - Ⓒ strings

2. A **Little Mary** is _____.
   - Ⓐ a hand puppet
   - Ⓑ a marionette
   - Ⓒ a rod puppet

3. You make a marionette move by pulling on _____.
   - Ⓐ the head
   - Ⓑ the arms
   - Ⓒ the strings

Bonus: Draw a marionette. Give your marionette a name.

Name _____

A Famous Person

Write the important details about the famous person's life.

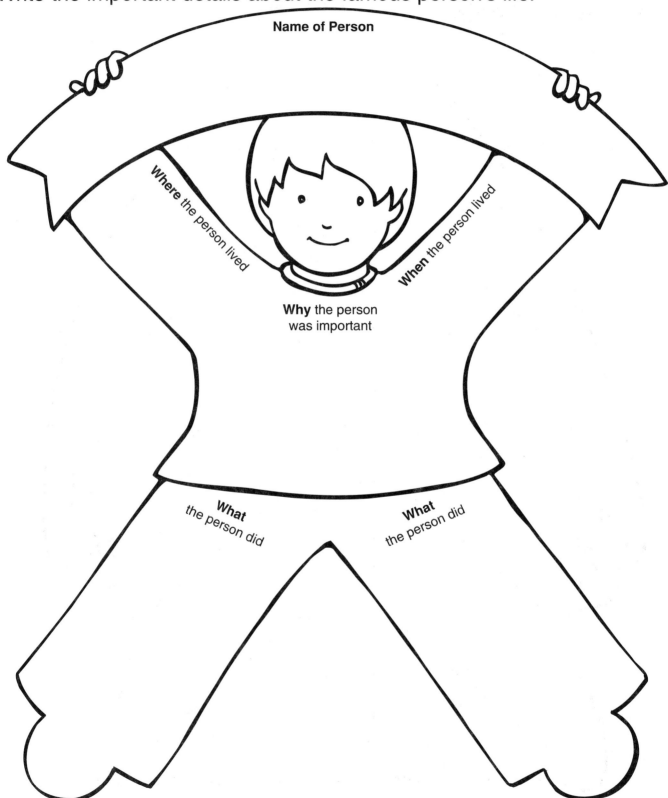

Name of Person

Where the person lived

When the person lived

Why the person was important

What the person did

What the person did

Nonfiction Reading Practice, Grade 1 • EMC 3312 • ©2003 by Evan-Moor Corp.

Name _____

Fishbone Diagram

Write the main idea of the article on the fish's spine. Write the details between the other bones.

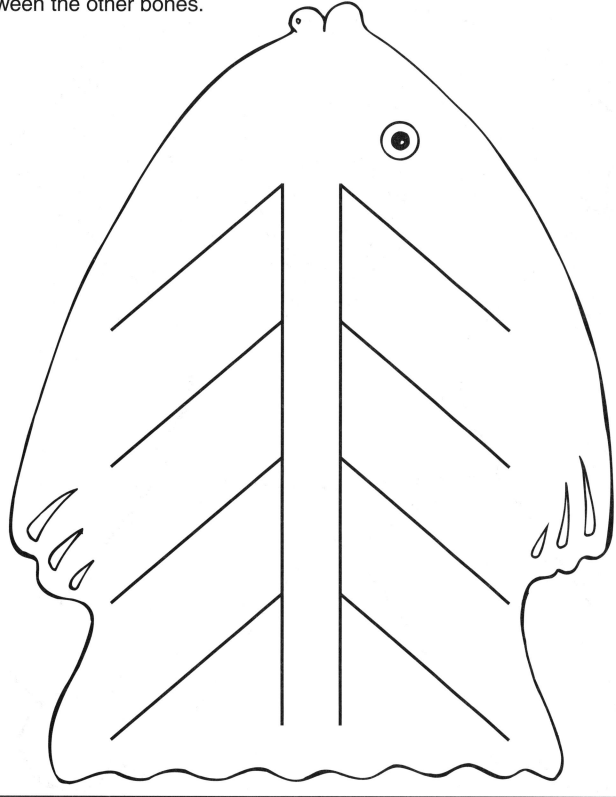

Note: This page may be reproduced for student use.

Name ____________________

Topic

____

K	What I **K**now
W	What I **W**ant to Know
L	What I **L**earned

Name _____

Sequence Chart

Put the events of the article
in the correct order.

1

2

3

4

5

Name _____

Spider Web

Write the topic of the article in the center of the web. Write details about the topic in the sections of the web.

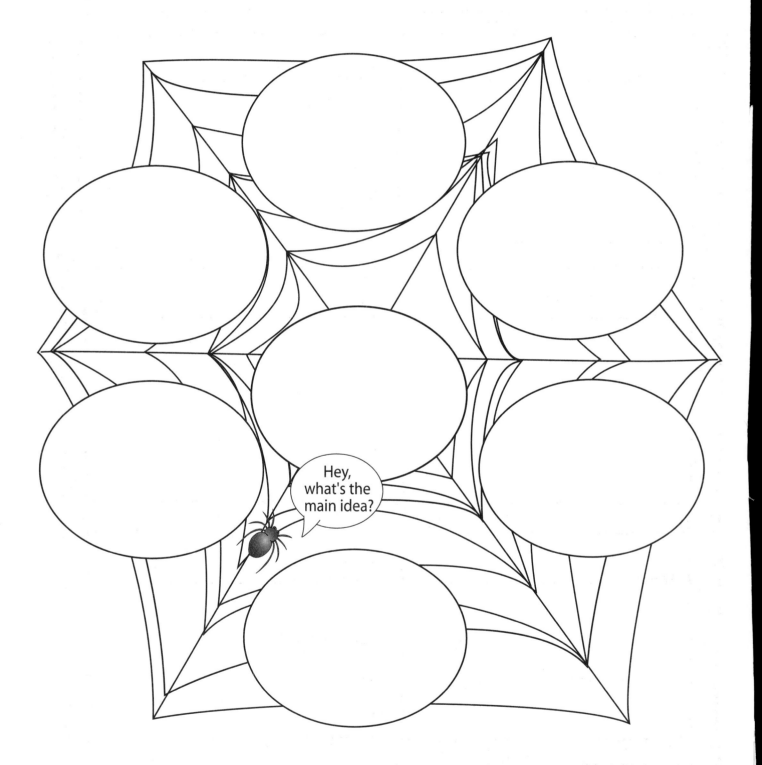

Nonfiction Reading Practice, Grade 1 • EMC 3312 • ©2003 by Evan-Moor Corp.

Name _____

Word Quilt

Write a new word you have learned in each quilt square. Write or draw what the word means in each quilt square.

Word: _____

Word: _____

Word: _____

Word: _____

Word: _____

Word: _____

Answer Key

page 9
1. B
2. C
3. B

Bonus: Answers will vary, but must be about a toy from today.

page 11
1. C
2. C
3. B

Bonus: Answers will vary. Students may write questions about any topic set in the past.

page 13
1. A
2. B
3. C

Bonus: Answers will vary, but students must choose the past or the future. They should give reasons why they would like to visit that period.

page 17
1. B
2. C
3. A

Bonus: Answers will vary.

page 19
1. A
2. C
3. B

Bonus: Answers will vary, but may include using the computer, listening to storytellers, or checking out books.

page 21
1. B
2. A
3. A

Bonus: Answers will vary. Students may show library workers doing such things as selecting books, conducting a story hour, or answering the phone.

page 25
1. B
2. A
3. C

Bonus: Answers will vary. Students may draw shapes for various areas and park equipment.

page 27
1. B
2. C
3. A

Bonus: Answers will vary, but must show things such as a bed, dresser, toy box, and closet.

page 29
1. A
2. B
3. A

Bonus: Answers will vary, but may include any natural or manmade areas.

page 33
1. B
2. C
3. A

Bonus: Answers will vary, but must relate to a brave deed.

page 35
1. B
2. C
3. A

Bonus: Answers will vary, but may include a friend, family member, acquaintance, or someone the student has read or heard about.

page 37
1. A
2. C
3. A

Bonus: Answers will vary. Students may write about the family of Pocahontas, her relationship with the settlers, and so on.

Nonfiction Reading Practice, Grade 1 • EMC 3312 • ©2003 by Evan-Moor Corp.

page 41
1. C
2. B
3. A

Bonus: Answers will vary, but should show one flat object and one 3-D shape.

page 43
1. A
2. B
3. A

Bonus: Answers will vary, but may include loading docks at a warehouse or store, wheelchair ramps in public buildings, portable ramps for moving vans, and so on.

page 45
1. B
2. A
3. B

Bonus: Answers will vary, but may include questions about the Nile, farming, the pyramids, and so on.

page 49
1. C
2. A
3. B

Bonus: Answers will vary, but must be a human habitat.

page 51
1. A
2. B
3. C

Bonus: Answers will vary. Students may write about insects, birds, fish, and wildlife that are native to the area.

page 53
1. B
2. A
3. C

Bonus: Answers will vary, but may include the areas mentioned in the article or others.

page 57
1. A
2. C
3. B

Bonus: Answers will vary. Students may select familiar solids or liquids from home or school.

page 59
1. A
2. C
3. B

Bonus: Answers will vary, but must be a food that can be changed from one matter to another.

page 61
1. C
2. A
3. C

Bonus: Answers will vary, but must include all forms—liquid, solid, and gas.

page 65
1. B
2. A
3. C

Bonus: Answers will vary.

page 67
1. B
2. B
3. A

Bonus: Answers will vary. Questions may include such things as what it looked like, how it felt, or the climate on the moon.

page 69
1. C
2. A
3. C

Bonus: Answers will vary, but may include details about what Neil saw and how he felt.

page 73

1. C
2. B
3. A

Bonus: Answers will vary, but must show proper clothing in each box.

page 75

1. A
2. B
3. C

Bonus: Answers will vary, but may include checking body temperature or outdoor temperature.

page 77

1. C
2. A
3. B

Bonus: Answers will vary, but may include items such as a measuring cup, ruler, or growth chart.

page 81

1. A
2. B
3. C

Bonus: Answers will vary, but should show an activity appropriate to a sunny day.

page 83

1. B
2. A
3. A

Bonus: Answers will vary. Students' drawings may include swirling colors. The sentence should describe the sun in some way that may include its temperature, its shape, its distance from Earth, or that it is a star.

page 85

1. C
2. A
3. B

Bonus: Answers will vary, but should include ideas that the planet would be cold and dark because it is far away from the sun.

page 89

1. B
2. C
3. C

Bonus: Answers will vary, but should include details about being safe at play.

page 91

1. C
2. B
3. C

Bonus: Answers will vary, but may include excuses for not turning in homework, having a messy bedroom, forgetting to feed a pet, or other scenarios.

page 93

1. C
2. C
3. B

Bonus: Answers will vary, but may include items such as wrist and knee pads, goggles, boots, gloves, coats, masks, oven mitts, sunglasses, steel-toed shoes, or bright colors for joggers.

page 97

1. C
2. A
3. A

Bonus: Answers will vary, but need to relate to a visit to the doctor.

page 99

1. B
2. B
3. C

Bonus: Answers will vary, but must refer his inventing a new vaccine to help prevent polio.

page 101

1. B
2. A
3. A

Bonus: Answers will vary. Students may mention family members, friends, community helpers, or celebrities they especially admire.

page 105
1. A
2. C
3. C

Bonus: Answers will vary.

page 107
1. C
2. A
3. B

Bonus: Answers will vary. Students may suggest any song that has a verse or chorus that can be sung in about 15 seconds. (Allow them to time their choices.)

page 109
1. A
2. B
3. C

Bonus: Answers will vary, but should include three rules such as washing hands after sneezing, after playing with a pet, and after playing outdoors.

page 113
1. C
2. A
3. C

Bonus: Answers will vary.

page 115
1. A
2. B
3. A

Bonus: Answers will vary, but may include such things as toys, clothes, or food items.

page 117
1. C
2. B
3. C

Bonus: Answers will vary. Students should name their new kind of money.

page 121
1. A
2. C
3. B

Bonus: Answers will vary, but must show some type of clock.

page 123
1. A
2. B
3. C

Bonus: Answers will vary, but may include having a snack, playing outside, doing homework, watching TV, and so on.

page 125
1. B
2. A
3. B

Bonus: Answers will vary, but students must choose one kind of clock and give reasons why they like it.

page 129
1. B
2. B
3. B

Bonus: Answers will vary. Students should give reasons why they particularly enjoy that day of the week.

page 131
1. B
2. A
3. C

Bonus: Answers will vary, but may include home, school, and community activities.

page 133
1. C
2. A
3. C

Bonus: Answers will vary, but may include holidays, appointments, project due dates, special activities, and so on.

page 137
1. B
2. C
3. A

Bonus: Answers will vary, but must show the child and a pet.

page 139
1. B
2. A
3. A

Bonus: Answers will vary, but may include a family activity, a special celebration, learning to do something new, or creating something.

page 141
1. C
2. A
3. C

Bonus: Drawings and stories will vary. Students might choose a special birthday party, birth of a sibling, or their pet.

page 145
1. A
2. A
3. C

Bonus: Answers will vary. Students may describe the song or write the actual words.

page 147
1. B
2. A
3. C

Bonus: Answers will vary. Students may write about friends, relatives, or pen pals who live in other cities, states, or countries.

page 149
1. B
2. C
3. C

Bonus: Answers will vary. Encourage students to make up a tune for their song and sing it to a friend.

page 153
1. B
2. C
3. C

Bonus: Answers will vary, but must show a house.

page 155
1. B
2. A
3. C

Bonus: Answers will vary, but encourage students to be creative.

page 157
1. B
2. A
3. A

Bonus: Answers will vary, but encourage students to be creative.

page 161
1. C
2. A
3. B

Bonus: Answers will vary, but may include a favorite toy puppet or one they have seen on TV or another theater show.

page 163
1. C
2. B
3. A

Bonus: Answers will vary. Students may write about a homemade or purchased puppet they played with at home, school, or at a friend's house.

page 165
1. A
2. B
3. C

Bonus: Answers will vary, but students should include strings on the marionette and name it.